"John Ramirez writes an unprecedented book about spiritual warfare—having gone way deep into the occult, now fully saved, undeniably called and ignited by the Holy Spirit. Read this book carefully. Learn from John's experiences and wisdom. Most importantly, never be complacent again about spiritual warfare, the occult and your powerful authority in Jesus Christ."

Jennifer Eivaz, executive pastor, Harvest
Christian Center, Turlock, California;
founder, Harvest Ministries International;
author, *The Intercessors Handbook*
and *Seeing the Supernatural*

"John's life message is the destruction of the works of darkness—a message the world needs today more than ever. Our kids need to know and learn the contents of this book. *Armed and Dangerous* is full of daily life skills that will help you disarm any work the enemy could ever think of bringing your way. I encourage you to add this book to your personal library as an available resource to prepare and equip you in spiritual warfare."

Nicky Cruz, evangelist and bestselling author

ARMED
AND DANGEROUS

ARMED
AND DANGEROUS

THE ULTIMATE BATTLE PLAN
FOR TARGETING AND DEFEATING THE ENEMY

JOHN
RAMIREZ

Chosen
a division of Baker Publishing Group
Minneapolis, Minnesota

Published by Chosen Books
11400 Hampshire Avenue South
Bloomington, Minnesota 55438
www.chosenbooks.com

Chosen Books is a division of
Baker Publishing Group, Grand Rapids, Michigan

Printed in the United States of America

Library of Congress Control Number: 2017941810

ISBN 978-0-8007-9850-5

"In Dreams and Visions" and "'You're Unworthy'—The Devil's Lie" by David Wilkerson used by permission of World Challenge, Inc., PO Box 260, Lindale, TX 75771, www.worldchallenge.org.

Unless otherwise indicated, Scripture quotations are from the King James Version of the Bible.

Scripture quotations identified ESV are from The Holy Bible, English Standard Version® (ESV®), copyright © 2001 by Crossway, a publishing ministry of Good News Publishers. Used by permission. All rights reserved. ESV Text Edition: 2011

Scripture quotations identified NASB are from the New American Standard Bible®, copyright © 1960, 1962, 1963, 1968, 1971, 1972, 1973, 1975, 1977, 1995 by The Lockman Foundation. Used by permission. (www.Lockman.org)

Scripture quotations identified NIV are from the Holy Bible, New International Version®. NIV®. Copyright © 1973, 1978, 1984, 2011 by Biblica, Inc.™ Used by permission of Zondervan. All rights reserved worldwide. www.zondervan.com

Scripture quotations identified NKJV are from the New King James Version®. Copyright © 1982 by Thomas Nelson, Inc. Used by permission. All rights reserved.

Scripture quotations identified NLT are from the Holy Bible, New Living Translation, copyright © 1996, 2004, 2015 by Tyndale House Foundation. Used by permission of Tyndale House Publishers, Inc., Carol Stream, Illinois 60188. All rights reserved.

Cover Design by Rob Williams

Author is represented by Leticia Gomez, Savvy Literary Services, and Raoul Davis, Director of Ascendant Publishing

18 19 20 21 22 23 24   11 10 9 8 7 6 5

I dedicate this book to
all the wonderful believers
who have written to John Ramirez Ministries
in spiritual pain.

I am standing with you all in prayer
on the battlefield.
There is victory in Jesus Christ.

Amen.

Contents

Foreword 11
Acknowledgments 13
Introduction: A Letter from Heaven 15

1. The Unarmed Church 21
2. Valley of Dry Bones 27
3. Beginnings: Good vs. Evil 37
4. Subtle Infiltration 45
5. Unveiling the Unholy Curtain: No. 21 63
6. Who Owns the Remote Control of Your Mind? 83
7. Destroying the Patterns and Cycles of the Evil One 91
8. Get Your Ph.D. in Spiritual Warfare 105
9. Fighting Back with Our God-Given Authority in Jesus 119
10. How to Take Back Lost Turf 127
11. Keeping Your Rhythm in the Fight 137

12. Spiritual Warfare Prayer Guide for Everyday Life   145

13. My Alabaster Box   161

14. Waiting on God When It Seems He Has Passed You By   185

15. Living Armed and Dangerous   195

Foreword

I was one of eighteen children born to witchcraft-practicing parents from Puerto Rico, so bloodshed and mayhem were common occurrences in my life. I suffered severe physical and mental abuse at their hands, at one time being declared the "Son of Satan" by my mother while she was in a spiritual trance.

When I was fifteen, my father sent me to visit my older brother in New York. I did not stay with my brother long. Instead, full of anger and rage, I chose to make it on my own. No authority figure could reach me—until I met a skinny street preacher named David Wilkerson. He disarmed me, showing me something I had never known before: relentless love.

The gospel message I was presented with during those early days has gripped my life and still grips me to this day. I am living proof that God can change any heart and that it is never too late.

John Ramirez and I met when he was attending and serving at Times Square Church in New York City. I was there to preach when we were introduced. I found it interesting that like me, John had been raised in a witchcraft-practicing family. And John had also been declared a "Son of Satan."

John's life message is the destruction of the works of darkness—a message the world needs today more than ever. Our kids need to know and learn the contents of this book, *Armed and Dangerous.*

Armed and Dangerous is full of daily life skills that will help you disarm any work the enemy could ever think of bringing your way. These things are rarely talked about in other places, as John speaks from an insider's perspective, having been involved in the Satanic Church. In today's culture of spiritual battles, which is everywhere we look, the battle is at hand and it is on your doorstep. It is in the classrooms, it is in the home and it is everywhere in our culture. A battle that will require battle weapons, battle words and a battle-tested life.

I encourage you to add this book to your personal library as an available resource to prepare and equip you in spiritual warfare.

Nicky Cruz, evangelist and bestselling author

Acknowledgments

I thank God with every breath I take for saving me, delivering me and depositing in me the Holy Spirit. Every day I open my eyes to the gift that the Holy Spirit is within me; He has kept me close throughout the years of this amazing walk. I thank God with all my heart for my second chance in life.

I want to thank God for my precious mother, Esther Martinez. At one time in our lives we were so far apart, but today, because of God's love, we are like peanut butter and jelly—we go together. My mother is seventy years old, and she said she could not be any prouder of me than she is for what God has done in my life. On her iPad, she watches every televised moment of the ministry God has given me. Thank you, Mom. You are a superstar.

I want to share my love to all the churches that have given me the opportunity to be a part of their lives and ministries. I hold you all dear to my heart, and I thank God for you.

I am grateful to Chosen Books for the opportunity to put this book together, with the help of Jesus Christ, to bless the world. I would also like to thank my two wonderful agents,

Raoul and Leticia, for believing in the calling that has been placed on my life. They are visionaries and they saw the hand of God upon my life. I thank Jesus for you both.

I am grateful and thankful to my spiritual overseers, Pastors Alex and Sandra Sarraga at Champions Ministries in Orlando, Florida, for the incredible love they have for me.

I also thank God for my home church, Times Square Church. The powerful preaching blesses my spirit and keeps me on track in my walk with God.

I praise Jesus Christ for the wonderful people I am about to name. They have ministered to my life in many ways. I want to thank the partners who provide for John Ramirez Ministries with prayer and financial support. You mean the world to me. I want to extend a thank you to Denise Loffredo. She is an incredible woman of God and super anointed, and I am grateful to her for typing up this book and for running the administrative work of my ministry without skipping a beat. I thank God for you every day.

I thank Cheryl Usher for her diligent work of running my social media with excellence. I thank God for you.

I also want to extend my love and appreciation to my longtime friend, Angie Kiesling, for teaming up with me to edit this amazing book. I am so proud of her for beating the devil down in getting her victory, through Jesus Christ, of defeating cancer. You are a champion in Jesus.

There are special people who played a part in my personal and spiritual life through Christian-based TV programs and radio shows, like Shannon Davis from Omega-Man Radio, and many others. I am eternally grateful for every one of you.

And above all, I am grateful for our Master Messiah, Jesus Christ.

Introduction

A Letter from Heaven

In every generation, God raises up a person to address and confront the spiritual attacks of that time. We read in the Bible how God raised up David to deal with Goliath, God raised up Moses to deal with Pharaoh and God raised up Esther to deal with the Hitler of her generation.

I believe in my heart that the Lord Jesus Christ has raised me up to deal with the enemy and his kingdom of darkness to bring a supernatural awakening to the body of Christ in the 21st century.

Rude Awakening

After years of serving the devil, I became a born-again believer in Christ—and it was the best thing that ever happened to me. I bought a big fat Bible, put index tabs on its pages and, with my marching song on, went off to church excited every week. My game plan was to take piano lessons and join any worship team that would have me. I even bought maracas and played them in church for a while. Life was good and my future seemed bright.

Then I got the "memo from heaven," as I have come to think of it, that my plan was not the same as God's game plan for me. For more than two years, I felt like Jeremiah when he said that God had deceived him (see Jeremiah 20:7). The memo told me that God had called me to be a radical evangelist and that I would be His arrow in His quiver to expose and destroy the works of darkness. I would be on the frontline of spiritual warfare.

I received confirmation that God was not confused about my calling when sometime later a phone call came in from another believer. His name was Shannon Davis, and he hosted a frontline radio ministry of deliverance. Shannon asked me to be on his show to share my testimony. I thought the invitation was a one-shot deal so I agreed to it. But God was setting me up.

After the radio program, Shannon continued sending me CDs about casting out devils. He kept saying, "Dude, God has called you to the frontline of spiritual warfare deliverance."

I thought he was crazy, a loose cannon. In my heart I was saying, *I've got my own plan. I'm going to play the piano and go to church*, when I could not play the piano if my life depended on it.

My awesome brother Shannon did not stop sending packages and calling me to talk about demons and spiritual warfare—not even once. Every time I received CDs from him, I would put them on top of my refrigerator with my Double Stuf Oreos. Whenever he would call and ask, "Hey, did you listen to the CDs?" I would reply, "Yeah, I'm real close to listening to them," while saying to myself, *Yeah, right.*

I found out much later that my arms were too short to box with God. I said out loud, "Lord, come on. I did 25 years of devil worshiping, and now You're going to put me in this battle?" I did not want anything more to do with demons. I was mad at God for a very long time after that, but I also knew that, like Jeremiah, I had a fire in my bones that would not be quenched—and that spiritual warfare was my calling.

Since 1999, I have been confronting and exposing the works of darkness and helping people around the world know the freedom paid for by Jesus' sacrifice.

Offense Wins Championships

One of the things that baffles my mind is how impotent the Church has become in the face of rampant evil. We have lost our fight. Let me give you a stark contrast to this failure: In my 25 years in the occult, I was trained to be a general, a force to be reckoned with in the spirit world to dismantle and destroy anything that threatened the kingdom of darkness.

It saddens me as a follower of Jesus that the Church has neglected its calling to be armed and dangerous. Where are the generals? We are called to wage spiritual warfare at the highest level. Because we are seated with Jesus Christ in the highest heavens, in a position of authority, we are equipped to kick in the gates of hell (see Ephesians 2:6). But we have left our posts. The Church has neglected to destroy the fiery darts of the evil one.

David said to the Lord, "Blessed be the LORD my Rock, who trains my hands for war, and my fingers for battle" (Psalm 144:1 NKJV), and also, "He makes my feet like hinds' feet, and sets me upon my high places. He trains my hands for battle, so that my arms can bend a bow of bronze" (Psalm 18:33–34 NASB). David was saying that the Lord was teaching him *offense* so he could destroy anything in front of him that opposed his walk with God and his purpose and destiny.

You may say, *John, what is offense?* I am glad you asked. Offense is to be spiritually aggressive and consistent in opposing the fiery darts of the enemy without hesitation, without losing ground in our faith, and then pushing forward.

When I served in Satan's kingdom, we were never taught defense. Instead, we were taught offense because whoever strikes first has the upper hand. This means whoever positions himself first in the battle will be immovable.

Let me give you an example. As it is in the natural, so it is in the spirit realm. I remember back when I was big into watching boxing on TV, and I especially remember boxer Mike Tyson. Tyson was a force to be reckoned with. He was the kind of boxer who, even before he got into the ring, had already beat you in his mind. To his thinking, he had already won the fight. So much so that when he went into the ring, many fights did not go past the first round. He would unleash fury on his opponent. He believed that offense was more powerful than defense.

Conquering Your Promised Land

There is an amazing story in the Old Testament about how God displayed His awesome power by visiting ten plagues upon Pharaoh and the Egyptian army that had been keeping the Israelites captive—and His display was undeniable. God had made a promise to the Israelites that He would take them into a land flowing with milk and honey. It was called the Promised Land.

Only one problem: The land was already occupied. How amazing that God will promise you a victory, but you must go and fight for it—even though the victory is already won. It sounds like an oxymoron. Not only is God testing your faith, to see if you take Him at His word, but He wants to see if you, too, will step out in faith to accomplish the mission.

As the Israelites went out and fought for their land, their God-given territory, so it is today for believers in Jesus. Today, we as the Church have been given a promise for the cause of Christ, and we must fight for our Promised Land. We fight for our purpose, our destiny, our salvation, our families, our loved ones and even for the unbelievers in the world so they, too, can have an opportunity to make it to the cross. We are soldiers and ambassadors of an army so elite that words cannot adequately describe it. In the coming chapters, I will teach you how to fight spiritually as a part of this elite army.

God has not called us to be a Moses generation that dies in the desert, yet many churches today are dying in the wilderness of their calling. Every month, pastors by the hundreds are closing churches because the devil has worried them—and they refuse to fight back.

One thing I have learned in my life of walking with Jesus is that storms do not last. Often in the battle I feel like the woman with the issue of blood—spiritually weak at times, exhausted in a hundred ways, even tasting discouragement. But I have learned to push my way through in the power of the Holy Spirit, touch the hem of His garment and get my victory. In my crazy thinking as a young believer, I signed a vow to the Lord in 1999 that read: *I'm doing life in Jesus Christ, and I want no parole.*

I am in it to win it and I am in it for life.

When Jesus Christ wakes me up every morning, I know the devil is in trouble. I am God's secret weapon. And so are you. Let us thank Jesus together. Thank You, Jesus!

As the Church of Jesus Christ, many of us are sitting with our hands folded or wishfully thinking that the devil will go away. We may even bring our situation into pity parties— thank God this is not the case in all churches. But for the Church, it is time to take a stand. No more patty-cake with the devil.

Later in this book you will learn how to understand the patterns and cycles of the evil one against your life, and how to dismantle and destroy them.

Because we are the Church of Jesus Christ, God has called us to be spiritual snipers and bring it to the devil like he has never seen before. We have the authority and the mandate to destroy his works because "the Son of God appeared for this purpose, to destroy the works of the devil" (1 John 3:8 NASB).

Are you ready to fight?

The Unarmed Church

The ultimate question I always ask myself is this: Why are believers in the Lord Jesus Christ taking such a pounding from the forces of darkness?

It should not be this way. In my travels around the world I have seen something that disturbs me and saddens my heart. Again and again, I see the Church in this dark condition. When Jesus Christ said at the cross, "It is finished," He gave us the victory (see John 19:30). But what I see is a Church lying bleeding on the battlefield.

The early Church in the book of Acts was a force to be reckoned with spiritually. The Church was respected and held in high regard. Hell trembled when it heard the names of the apostles.

Jesus has given us everything we need to be victorious against the wicked schemes that the enemy and his cronies throw at us. When Jesus told Peter that the gates of hell will not prevail against His Church, it was settled (see Matthew 16:18). Why have we, and the Church-at-large, cowered from this calling and tried to be politically and spiritually correct instead? Could it be that we are overdosing on the study of theology, or focusing too much on spirituality, yet in denial about the power that we carry in Jesus?

The apostle Paul wrote to his spiritual son Timothy about people who have "a form of godliness, but denying the power thereof," warning him, "from such turn away" (2 Timothy 3:5). He could have been writing about many of us.

Why do we deny the power that we carry in Jesus? Why are we so afraid to talk about the devil, or expose him, or even talk about spiritual warfare? We act like we are committing blasphemy against the Holy Spirit and walk on eggshells, as if we, the Church, have committed the ultimate sin.

The devil has put that fear in the Church today. Do you really think that if you do not expose the devil or talk about spiritual warfare, the enemy will not mess with you? Think again.

Let us wake up and be the true Church of Jesus Christ: armed and dangerous.

Innocence Lost

I have not always felt such a love for the Church. My complete testimony appears in *Out of the Devil's Cauldron* (Heaven and Earth Media, 2012), but it is important for you to know there was a time in my life when I hated the Church, hated God and hated anything to do with His Son, Jesus Christ.

As a strong believer today, having served Jesus Christ for many years, I often reflect on and rejoice in the goodness of the Lord—how He put the pieces of my fragmented life back together. He took a great mess and made it His masterpiece, and He called His masterpiece evangelist John Ramirez. God always gives us beauty for ashes.

My descent into witchcraft, however, began innocently. Like any other little boy living in the South Bronx of the 1960s, I played among the rubble of burned-out buildings that decayed the beauty of the neighborhood. On one particular broken and dilapidated lot, my best friend and I loved to play "who can throw the rock the farthest," breaking windows—and laughing out loud when we scored a hit.

One day, as my friend and I broke window after window, time passing quickly, an eerie sense overtook me. I felt a heavy presence but did not know what it was and tried to shake it off.

Suddenly, something hit my feet, and I stooped down to find a colorful necklace on the ground. I did not realize it then, but that necklace—which resembled Native American art—was my first encounter with the dark side. A short time later, the necklace, which was connected to an unspeakable evil, would steal my childhood.

Months later, I was on my way to see a witch.

Two Baptisms

Given my demonic past, one thing I am so thankful to Jesus for today is my water baptism as a new believer in Him. That day more than two hundred people filled the sanctuary, and of the fifty new believers who came to be baptized, I was the last one. As I walked up on stage and was led to the baptism pool, I received the most incredible standing ovation ever—those precious saints, many who barely knew me, cheered because they knew what God had delivered me from.

Though my heart rejoiced, my mind went back to a distant day, to the unholy baptism I was subjected to as a little boy just a few months after finding the strange necklace on the broken lot.

On that day, the scene was very different.

Instead of a church full of praising saints, I walked into a dingy apartment filled with demons.

Instead of the holy waters of baptism, I experienced an herbal bath with demonic chanting in the background.

My aunt had persuaded my mother to go for a tarot card reading, and I ended up in the crossfire. The medium singled me out as her demonic protégé, and before my mother and I knew what was happening, I was being ushered into the dark side.

My discipleship with the devil would last 25 years.

A Dark Deception

No longer that innocent little boy who threw rocks at vacant windows, I had grown into a tall young man who dressed all in black (or white if the spirits called for it) and who strode through the streets of the Bronx with a proud swagger. Seeing people recognize me and hurry inside their doorways, not wanting to make eye contact with me—the devil's son—gave me a secret thrill.

I was handpicked by the devil himself to be a high priest in the demonic realm, and the priesthood ceremony took place one night in the basement of my aunt's house.

At five minutes to midnight, the devil showed up to collect the debt on his contract. The ritual lasted into the wee hours of the night, and the next morning, when I woke up on the basement floor, I was no longer John Ramirez.

As a general in Satan's kingdom, I was ordered to curse and control regions, do blood rituals and basically bring hell to earth. I was also an evangelist for the dark side, recruiting any gullible soul I could find. My favorite targets were weak Christians. That was my world.

Colliding with the Cross

After years of walking in darkness so profound it would shock you, I was invited to church by a new girlfriend—and I went. To me it was a big joke. Who invites the devil's son to church? I never imagined that God had a sense of humor and He would have the last laugh.

I continued to attend that church with her, privately deriding the experience, until an October night changed my life forever—in a larger-than-life dream that would lead me on the right path to eternity. It was a dream that God used to show me He was bigger and more powerful than anything I had served for 25 years in the world of witchcraft.

Sometimes we have to walk through the broken neighborhoods to get to the healthy neighborhood. It took a visit to hell before I could reach heaven.

After waking up from that vivid dream, I cried out to God, saying, "You *are* real and You do love me. Despite everything I said against You, how I mocked You and laughed at Your Church, how I ridiculed Christians, trying to break their faith—in spite of all this, You still love me. Jesus, I give my life to You. I will serve You instead of the demons, and You will be Lord over my life. You are the true God."

Then I took out a piece of paper, marking the date in 1999, and wrote a vow to the Lord promising to serve Him and to be fully surrendered to His will for the rest of my life.

Jesus Christ had delivered me from witchcraft. Never again to return.

Valley of Dry Bones

The late David Wilkerson used to say that God will "baptize you in anguish" so you can understand His heartbeat for His Church. It is an amazing experience, yet something you must ask for.

In my early years as a believer I would sit in Times Square Church and hear Pastor David talk about all the email that came into his ministry. He described how many good-hearted believers in Jesus Christ were going through the storms of their lives, such as sickness from cancer, families destroyed through addictions, divorce, lack of forgiveness, witchcraft and so forth. When he made the statement about being baptized in anguish, I did not understand it at the time.

Today God has baptized me in anguish, and now I fully understand what Pastor David—a man with a golden heart for the Church—meant.

I feel this same burden for my brothers and sisters in the Body of Christ. This is one reason why I wrote this book: to impact and help as many believers as I can, through the power of the Holy Spirit.

When I was on the other side in Satan's kingdom, I would have rejoiced at what believers are going through today. Now I will stand in the gap for anyone who puts their trust in Jesus. I will share the battlefield with you and believe the Lord Jesus Christ for your victory.

Let me share my heart with you: The condition of the Church today reminds me of the prophet Ezekiel's valley of dry bones. This amazing account in the Old Testament tells about an incredible group of people who were handpicked by God, but somehow lost their way and ended up spiritually dry and thirsty, unable to find their way back to the perfect will of God.

> The Lord took hold of me, and I was carried away by the Spirit of the Lord to a valley filled with bones. He led me all around among the bones that covered the valley floor. They were scattered everywhere across the ground and were completely dried out.
>
> Ezekiel 37:1–2 NLT

Although this chapter in Ezekiel refers to the nation of Israel, it also applies symbolically to how God will raise up a watchman on the wall to speak to the compromising Church, the Church that has lost its way—entangled in deception— and has often ended up in the enemy's camp.

Please do not misunderstand. I am not calling myself a watchman on the wall, but I *am* saying that someone *must* address the condition of the Church today—with love. Someone who really loves the Church of Jesus Christ.

There are times when we have to get radical. Take, for example, the account in the Old Testament of when David was running away from King Saul and ran straight into the Philistines' camp and became trapped. David found his way back to the place that God wanted him to be by acting like a madman so that the Philistine king would dismiss him (see 1 Samuel 21:10–13).

Let us get back to the account of the prophet Ezekiel:

> The LORD took hold of me, and I was carried away by the Spirit of the LORD to a valley filled with bones.
>
> Ezekiel 37:1 NLT

This group of people had experienced an incredible encounter with God Himself, yet through sin and disobedience, they ended up in a place of death. God has extraordinary mercy and love for us today. Yet as the compromised Church, if we do not take heed of the spiritual situations that are attacking us, if we take things lightly and do not hear the warning signs, we can end up in our own valley of dry bones.

Another story involving this same group of people in the book of Exodus reminds me so much of Christian believers today. The Israelites were in bondage for many years, a lot like we were before coming to Christ. These wonderful people saw the mighty hand of God move in Egypt the same way that God moved in our lives when we were still trapped in the enemy's camp. They saw the incredible power of God by the way He brought ten plagues on Egypt to set them free, against all odds. We, too, have seen the incredible hand of God in our lives, and He has set us free from our own Egypt.

God has so much for us today. Let us live our lives through these amazing examples so we do not fall into the same dry-bones condition.

Too many times we give in easily to the enemy instead of resisting him, being consistent in Christ, taking the offensive in the Holy Spirit and crushing the works of darkness. That is what it means to be armed and dangerous. If we have seen the mighty works God has done for us, just as the Israelites saw what God did for them, why are we allowing the enemy to own the real estate in our lives?

Chemical Spiritual Warfare

When a diabolical attack hit me for a short season, it was like nothing I had ever seen before. Not even in all my years of devil worshiping.

This is a warning to the Church today that an attack is on its way and aimed straight for the Body of Christ. This warning is not meant to frighten you, but to prepare you for the battle with all your heart. The Lord brought me to His Word to give me an illustration. Before I share that with you, I would like to tell you what I experienced.

When this attack hit, all strength drained out of me. I could not think or function—I felt something like a spiritual zombie. I lost all hope of spending time with the Lord or reading the Word. Even worship songs sounded foreign to me. My days felt like weeks and my weeks like months. I sat in the middle of nowhere spiritually, feeling utterly drained, full of despair and physically spent. Just getting up in the morning was a struggle. It was as if I had lain down and died spiritually, with no direction or strength to fight back.

One afternoon, while I was stopped in traffic in the Big Apple, I decided to call a precious woman of God to say hello. Our conversation allowed me to open up and tell her about my condition.

Her response blew me away: She was experiencing the same kind of attack. This very seasoned person in the Lord and in ministry told me she was afraid to share her condition with anyone because they would not understand; they would think she had lost her mind.

I said, "Welcome to the new attack that the devil is ready to unleash in the last days upon the Church." At that moment, the Lord gave me a name for it: Chemical Spiritual Warfare.

An account in the Word of God describes a similar situation. Jesus tells the parable of the ten virgins and how five were wise and five were foolish.

"Then the kingdom of heaven shall be likened to ten virgins who took their lamps and went out to meet the bridegroom. Now five of them were wise, and five were foolish. Those who were foolish took their lamps and took no oil with them, but the wise took oil in their vessels with their lamps. But while the bridegroom was delayed, they all slumbered and slept.

"And at midnight a cry was heard: 'Behold, the bridegroom is coming; go out to meet him!' Then all those virgins arose and trimmed their lamps. And the foolish said to the wise, 'Give us some of your oil, for our lamps are going out.' But the wise answered, saying, 'No, lest there should not be enough for us and you; but go rather to those who sell, and buy for yourselves.' And while they went to buy, the bridegroom came, and those who were ready went in with him to the wedding; and the door was shut.

"Afterward the other virgins came also, saying, 'Lord, Lord, open to us!' But he answered and said, 'Assuredly, I say to you, I do not know you.'

"Watch therefore, for you know neither the day nor the hour in which the Son of Man is coming."

Matthew 25:1–13 NKJV

Notice that all ten virgins dressed the same, looked the same and even carried the same lamp. The women, who represent members of the Church, all fell asleep. I felt the same lethargy when I was hit. What saved me—and five of the ten virgins—was the substance in my lamp. Oil represents the infilling of the Holy Spirit. The five wise virgins were strong in the Lord and spiritually mature, which brought them across the finish line.

Arrows in God's Quiver

Allow me to share with you how to prepare for the battle to be an overcomer in Christ Jesus.

"Be obedient to those who are your masters according to the flesh, with fear and trembling, in sincerity of heart, as to Christ, not with eyeservice, as men-pleasers, but as bond-servants of Christ, doing the will of God from the heart" (Ephesians 6:5–6 NKJV).

Here are seven arrows in God's quiver that will help us to be armed and dangerous, ready for the battle toward victory. (In the Bible, the number seven represents divine perfection.)

1. Be strong in the Lord and spiritually mature. To be strong in the Lord means being submitted completely to the Holy Spirit and to the Word of God in obedience.

2. Believe God's Word. We must show ourselves approved by living out the Word of God in obedience.

3. Learn how to pray violently. In other words, we are to pray with the fire of the Holy Spirit in our mouths. "And from the days of John the Baptist until now the kingdom of heaven suffereth violence, and the violent take it by force" (Matthew 11:12). Destroy everything that opposes your relationship with God. These kinds of prayers will give you the victory. Passive prayers against the enemy are not effective.

4. Identify the attack. Sometimes the devil will throw counterfeit attacks, such as a bad week at work. I call these spiritual diversions. You jump in the ring with it, become spiritually exhausted afterwards and then the real fight shows up.

5. Engage in a ministry of fire. The Word says our God is a consuming fire (see Hebrews 12:29). We need to agree with God in the battle, and burn down every blockage, bondage, roadblock and satanic wall that the enemy has built against us. We must use violent prayers every step of the way. There is no negotiation with the enemy of your soul.

6. Fear not. Fear is the biggest weapon that the enemy has mastered against the Church. Fear paralyzes and brings torment into the battle. Satan is like a dog. He can smell fear in any believer. Spiritual warfare has zero tolerance for becoming afraid. Trust in the Lord.

7. Fast. Remember, before Jesus began His incredible ministry, He fasted for forty days and forty nights. "Then Jesus was led up by the Spirit into the wilderness to be tempted by the devil. And when He had fasted forty days

and forty nights, afterward He was hungry" (Matthew 4:1–2 NKJV).

The great apostle Paul began his ministry with three days of fasting. Fasting is like the oxygen we breathe. I call it spiritual oxygen. We must fast in order to be victorious when we confront spiritual weakness on any level. This discipline will carry you out from the valley of dry bones and into victory in Jesus Christ. Your armor might have some dents in it, but you will be a living testimony to other believers and to the world that the God you serve is great and greatly to be praised.

The devil is very limited in his power against true believers in Christ. Pastor David Wilkerson was a preacher beyond his time and a true prophet as well, touching millions of lives around the world. I leave you with a word that Pastor Wilkerson often shared with us in his amazing sermons at Times Square Church. It begins with the following Scripture verse:

> God is not a man, that he should lie; neither the son of man, that he should repent: hath he said, and shall he not do it? or hath he spoken, and shall he not make it good?
>
> Numbers 23:19

Reverend Wilkerson always preached that our Lord Jesus Christ was married to His Word. He also said that we can hold God to His Word, and admonished us to learn how to mix the Word with faith. Once you learn the principles of God's Word, you can hold Him to it. He does not mind. In fact, God delights in proving His faithfulness and loves when we speak the Word back to Him!

Apply His Word to every circumstance, every trial and every situation that you confront or that is opposing your blessing in your life. With every trial, every testing and every demonic attack, I came out on the other side with the victory. Always remember that no devil, no witch, no warlock or any demonic attack will be able to stand in your way. Meditate on this and take it to the bank. These are the promises God has given us, and they stand forever.

We are more than conquerors in Christ Jesus.

> Yet in all these things we are more than conquerors through Him who loved us.
>
> Romans 8:37 NKJV

The Word of the Lord says we are the head and not the tail.

> The LORD will make you the head, not the tail. If you pay attention to the commands of the LORD your God that I give you this day and carefully follow them, you will always be at the top, never at the bottom.
>
> Deuteronomy 28:13 NIV

We can do all things through Christ Jesus.

> I can do all things through Christ who strengthens me.
>
> Philippians 4:13 NKJV

Being an overcomer is our inheritance from our Lord Jesus Christ until the day that He returns. Bank on this.

Three Things the Devil Hates

Many Christians are oblivious about why the devil is so angry at us as believers in Christ. We need to understand his motives so we can fight the good fight of faith.

1. We are made in the image of God. When we find our true identity in Him who made us, we are unstoppable in the spirit realm. Every time the devil looks at us, it reminds him that he was crushed at the cross by Jesus Christ on behalf of the Father's children. We are the redeemed and the devil never will be.

2. We took his job. Satan led worship in heaven, and because of his rebellious ways he got fired and we got hired. Come to think of it, I would be angry, too, if someone stepped in and took my job. We are the true worshipers today and forevermore.

3. We can choose to walk in holiness. One of the greatest weapons you can use against the kingdom of darkness is to live a holy life in obedience to Christ. Holiness in the life of the believer is spiritual strength through the Holy Spirit, enabling you to live on the side of victory. The devil knows 100 percent that holiness is the greatest defense and offense against his wiles and schemes.

If you apply and live out these spiritual weapons in your Christian walk, you will never see a day in the valley of dry bones.

That does not mean you will not face the evil one. You will—you can count on it—but you will always have the victory.

Beginnings: Good vs. Evil

Do you ever wonder where Satan came from? His existence is not one of cartoon lore; he is not wearing a red suit and holding a pitchfork in his hand like Hollywood often portrays him. Satan's name was Lucifer until he was cast down to earth by God. Satan is often referred to as a fallen angel. He is the filthy one, and whoever makes allegiances with him will become the same way.

The passage of Scripture below gives an account of the battle of good and evil and what took place in heaven when Lucifer fell to the earth realm. Watch out! You have been warned.

"You were in Eden, the garden of God; every precious stone was your covering: the ruby, the topaz and the diamond; the beryl, the onyx and the jasper; the lapis lazuli, the turquoise and the emerald; and the gold, the workmanship of your settings and sockets, was in you. On the day that you were created they were prepared.

"You were the anointed cherub who covers, and I placed you there. You were on the holy mountain of God; you walked in the midst of the stones of fire.

"You were blameless in your ways from the day you were created until unrighteousness was found in you.

"By the abundance of your trade you were internally filled with violence, and you sinned; therefore I have cast you as profane from the mountain of God. And I have destroyed you, O covering cherub, from the midst of the stones of fire.

"Your heart was lifted up because of your beauty; you corrupted your wisdom by reason of your splendor. I cast you to the ground; I put you before kings, that they may see you.

"By the multitude of your iniquities, in the unrighteousness of your trade you profaned your sanctuaries. Therefore I have brought fire from the midst of you; it has consumed you, and I have turned you to ashes on the earth in the eyes of all who see you."

Ezekiel 28:13–18 NASB

The seventy returned with joy, saying, "Lord, even the demons are subject to us in Your name." And He said to them, "I was watching Satan fall from heaven like lightning. Behold, I have given you authority to tread on serpents and scorpions, and over all the power of the enemy, and nothing will injure you."

Luke 10:17–19 NASB

As we read in the Ezekiel passage, God created Lucifer as a beautiful, anointed cherub. He was adorned with precious jewels of all kinds, and he led worship in heaven. Now you know why music is so spiritually influential in the world, and how Satan has gotten his way through lyrics, and even in the beats and musical sounds.

Aware of his magnificence, Lucifer got puffed up with pride and decided to exalt himself and be like God—something he could never do, of course. The Lord God is God alone, perfect in righteousness and majesty, and He will not share His glory with anyone.

In the following passage, count how many times Lucifer says, "I will." (Remember, this self-centered pride was his downfall):

> "How you are fallen from heaven, O Day Star, son of Dawn! How you are cut down to the ground, you who laid the nations low! You said in your heart, 'I will ascend to heaven; above the stars of God I will set my throne on high; I will sit on the mount of assembly in the far reaches of the north; I will ascend above the heights of the clouds; I will make myself like the Most High.' But you are brought down to Sheol, to the far reaches of the pit."
>
> Isaiah 14:12–15 ESV

We need to choose our allegiances carefully. Which side do you want to be on, the side of righteousness or the side of self-will, self-righteousness and self-indulgence?

The Birth of Spiritual Warfare

When God kicked Satan out of heaven, he took one-third of the angels with him. These formerly holy angels became the evil spirits (demons) that do the devil's bidding. They war against the holy angels in the spirit realm, they influence and manipulate mankind toward evil and they especially war against the Church—despising all who align themselves with the cause of Christ.

Make no mistake—the devil is alive and well, and he operates primarily through systems of politics, the media and cultural traditions, dividing humanity against one another. He breeds hatred, division, discord and violence, and he afflicts humanity with diseases. He has held humanity captive and has taken their minds and fragmented their souls. Some people end up in prison because of his influence and the choices they make; others have ended up in mental wards and insane asylums, their minds hijacked by evil spirits.

Always understand there are two kingdoms mentioned in the Bible, and the line on the battlefield has been drawn between the two: the kingdom of darkness and the Kingdom of light. We must choose on which side we want to stand as believers. Thankfully, He has delivered us from the counterfeit kingdom of darkness.

The Bible makes it clear that we have won the victory over Satan and his evil kingdom through Jesus Christ. But we must not fall asleep because there is still a war raging for our souls. And we must be aware of who the enemy is and how he operates.

Take Inventory of Your Warehouse

First of all, who or what is your warehouse? It is you. And who owns the rights to your warehouse? Let us examine ourselves to see if there is any place within us that the enemy has been using to hold us captive. By unveiling and confronting the truth about what controls us, we can break free through Jesus Christ.

Circle any of the following attributes, experiences or afflictions that you have a problem with (or any involvement in):

Antichrist
Rebellion
Stubbornness
False prophet spirit

Anger
Rage
Wrath
Irrational anger
Temper
Violence

Bitterness
Hate
Self-hate
Lack of forgiveness
of self
Resentment
Revenge
Retaliation
Jealousy, envy
Murder

Bondage
Overbearing
Hyperactivity
Heaviness
Depression
Blocked emotion

Grief
Sorrow
Sadness
Hopelessness
Depression
Worry
Anxiety
Nervousness
Stress
Pressure
Tension
Self-pity
Despair
Loneliness
Disappointment

Idolatry / False Gods
Self
People
Things
Money
Sports
Business
Work
Social media
Lifestyle
Entertainment (TV, mov-
ies, etc.)

41

Jezebel
Seductive behavior
Witchcraft
Manipulation
Control

Mental Illness
Retardation
Schizophrenia
Bipolar disorder
Paranoia
Manic depression

Profanity
Cursing
Blasphemy
Taking God's name in vain

Religion
Traditions of men
False doctrines
Rituals
Legalism
Martial arts
Yoga
Secret societies (Freemasonry, Eastern Star, etc.)

Self
Selfishness
Self-gratification

Self-will
Self-righteousness

Strife
Conflict
Bickering
Argumentative
Quarreling
Fighting
Criticism
Judgmental
Gossiping
Accusations
Finding fault

Torment
Harassment
Nightmares

Witchcraft / Occult
Ouija boards
Familiar spirits
Spirit guides
Divination
Sorcery
Horoscopes, astrology
Fortune telling
Tarot cards
Worship of the dead
Charms, crystals

Voodoo
Wicca
Santeria
Spiritualism
Palo Mayombe
Medicine man spirit
Spiritual healer
Indian witchcraft
Shamanism
Psychics
Séance

Ungodly Soul Ties to Be Broken
Sexual groups (orgies)
Sexual abuse
Rape
Ex-husbands and ex-wives

Deception (Accepting Lies)
Self-deception
Delusional
Delirious
Blinding
Denial

Fear of
Death
Accidents
Future

Disapproval
Confrontation
Rejection
Darkness
Loneliness
Trust
Love
Commitment
Animals
Germs
Sickness
Satan
Going outside
Success
Panic attacks

Rejection
Self-rejection
Rejection in the womb

Perversion
Lust
Fantasies
Lesbianism
Homosexuality
Masturbation
Adultery
Molestation of children
Incest

Succubus	**Pride**
Incubus	Haughtiness
Harlot	Ego
Rape	Intellectualism
Bestiality	Vanity
Pornography	Self-righteousness
	Spiritual pride
Poverty	Ignorance
Financial bondage	
Financial blockage	
Financial destruction	

These are some of the fiery darts that the evil one will try to use to destroy our lives; if he cannot destroy us outright, he will work to keep us miserable and unproductive for the Kingdom of God. We need to be aware of these darts and check ourselves, allowing the Holy Spirit to search us so that none of these afflictions will be found in us.

Jesus said, "The thief does not come except to steal, and to kill, and to destroy. I have come that they may have life, and that they may have it more abundantly" (John 10:10 NKJV). We *can* live the life that God created for us. To do this we must stand on God's Word that says whom the Son sets free is free indeed.

Therefore if the Son makes you free, you shall be free indeed.

John 8:36 NKJV

Next, we will look at the sneaky ways the devil tries to infiltrate your life. Look out!

Subtle Infiltration

For 25 years, I had lost my way and spiraled into a person I no longer recognized. Yet thanks be to God, He saved me, set me free from bondage and then commissioned me to go and do likewise. As I mentioned previously, you can read my full story in my first book, *Out of the Devil's Cauldron* (Heaven and Earth Media). My task now is to train you how to be armed and dangerous—a lethal weapon in God's quiver.

In chapter one, I asked why believers in Jesus Christ have been taking such a pounding by forces of darkness. Stepping back, an even bigger question might be, How did the Church come to be so impotent? How did we get to this place of weak-kneed Christianity?

From the first-century Church until today, we have lost *our* way. We have become a mockery to the devil and to the world. We have become the medicated Church and the in-stitutional Church. Many churches today are teaching and preaching Jesus even when they no longer hear Jesus teaching and preaching to them. The word *Ichabod*—the glory of the Lord has departed—applies to many churches today, and the devil has taken over because we have lost our discernment.

The churches established by the apostles in first-century Palestine started off on fire. One hundred and twenty God-fearing people stepped out of the Upper Room onto the streets of Jerusalem just two weeks after Jesus' ascension to heaven—but they had a secret weapon. They had just been touched and soaked by the Holy Spirit.

Up till this time, the 120 had been hiding as marked men and women—with bull's-eyes on their backs—because they had decided to follow Jesus. But now, filled with the zeal and fire from the Holy Spirit, they took to the streets and were confronted by an angry mob filled with hate. That mob included the religious leaders, the very ones who had crucified Jesus.

Yet they were not afraid to confront the devil face-to-face. They understood how to engage demonic opposition with the Word of God. When three thousand souls were added to the Church in a single day, suddenly this powerful movement called Christianity was untouchable.

Fast-forward a few decades and already what started as a pure, on-fire Church had been infiltrated by the devil to water down the Gospel and pull people from the truth of Jesus Christ.

Today, we find ourselves in the same predicament. But a remnant is rising up, the end-time Church of Jesus Christ, and I thank God with all my heart for that. This remnant is ready to take on the last spiritual warfare fight that we will ever see. I believe that many will be set free, people will be healed and delivered from demonic oppression and every weapon in the devil's arsenal will be destroyed.

False Anointing and Cunning Perception

The devil has infiltrated the Church with corrupted gifts, especially in the area of leadership. In many churches, we have replaced the presence of God with the false gifts of people. Keep in mind that in my years as a devil worshiper, we, too, were into gifts that operated in the kingdom of darkness. Let me give you an example.

On Sunday mornings in many churches, we jump, we holler, we throw ourselves on the floor—we even do cartwheels around the church. The pastors or leaders get up to preach, but instead of relying on a true calling, they lean on their charismatic nature. They have learned how to work a crowd—often to a point of a spiritual high—because many have fallen in love with the gift instead of the presence of God.

The Church has become spiritually anemic. Without the presence of God, there is no spiritual substance, and we have let our guards down and turned the service of God into New Age–type gatherings, as if the Church has become a club.

In many churches, we have a Jezebel sitting in the front seat, and in some other assemblies, Delilah—a seducing spirit. The Church has lost its discernment. This is very difficult to write because it is not a popular concept, and no one wants to address the elephant in the room.

The Church or the World: Which One Are You?

Have you ever been enticed by something that appears fruitful yet is anything but? Every enticement tastes like honey, but turns bitter when it hits your stomach.

The devil knows just how to prey on us with such enticements. One way is to wrap up situations and circumstances

47

in an attractive suit called "good deeds." We are suckers for such enticements and can fall easily into the trap. One example was the Ice Bucket Challenge.

By now, most of us are likely familiar with the Ice Bucket Challenge and how this event ran like wildfire through churches and cities all over the world. A young man trying to raise money for a friend in need started the challenge, and rarely did anyone take notice or investigate the spirituality behind it. Instead, many of us embraced the challenge and participated.

This brings me to the question: Are we of the world or of the Church?

Let me share my heart with you. I was initiated into the witchcraft world with a demonic ceremony called Santi, which is a Haitian/French ritual demanded by demons that operate in those regions. To seal the deal or complete the contract, I participated in an all-day ceremony, moving from one ritual to another until the very end. The demons wanted to seal the ceremony because they knew this would give them legal rights over my life.

This common ritual consists of a bucket filled with ice-cold water, which is poured over the head to drench the initiate from head to toe, sealing the contract. I was part of that ceremony, but very few in the kingdom of darkness were chosen to partake of this evil act.

When the Ice Bucket Challenge became so popular a few years ago, I was shocked at how easily we embraced the devil's bait. Around the clock, people were challenging others to sign up for this despicable act. The last one laughing was the devil himself.

Later, the young man who co-founded the challenge died in a bizarre accident. What a tragedy for all. We have to be very careful about what we sign up for. I wonder how many were more excited to do the Ice Bucket Challenge than to take part in scriptural water baptism.

This is not to condemn anyone, but I do want to issue a wake-up call. If you did the Ice Bucket Challenge, you should renounce it in the name of Jesus and never give the devil the upper hand again.

The question may be asked, What if someone did this challenge innocently, not knowing its true origins? My answer, whether you did it consciously or unconsciously, is where did it fit the Word of God? Where did it fit your knowledge of Jesus Christ? The world will never bring anything holy to the Church. As believers, we should be sensitive to the Spirit's lead. When anything of the world is introduced to us, we should be able to discern the truth and say *no*, instead of saying *yes* and suffering the consequences.

Are we the Church, or are we the world? Where is our spiritual identity?

Let me share another situation with you.

Out of the Horse's Mouth

Anton LaVey, the founder of the Church of Satan, said: "I am glad that Christian parents let their children worship the devil at least one night out of the year. Welcome to Halloween."

I find it ironic that we are quick on our feet to rush and honor the devil in so many ways. We see no harm in Halloween, because we think it is fun. We paint our faces, we wear our innocent costumes, we dress up our doorways—even churches dress up their entryways for Halloween with pumpkins. These actions are like giving the devil license, saying, "Here's my church. You can have it."

We think that because that night we are not performing any demonic rituals or human sacrifices that we are on safe ground, but did you know that as soon as you dress up, whether you color yourself or put on a costume, the enemy owns you? Because by doing so, you have turned over your legal rights and you have dedicated yourself and your kids to celebrating the devil's holiday. You have just made a pact with the enemy, and you are already sacrificing your children spiritually by dressing them up and changing their identity.

Losing Our Identity

My mind goes back to the night of October 31, 1987, when I had the most diabolical wedding on the planet. My fiancée and I decided to get married on Halloween, in a demonic ritual that lasted all night, and the wedding bells were heard all the way down to the gates of hell.

That night, we forfeited our identity in return for a demonic, despicable wedding because we forgot, like everybody else who celebrates this holiday, to count the costs of our consequences. Like many of us today, we rushed into celebrating the devil's birthday, so to speak, and we thought it was fun. It is like the person who tries drugs for the first time because he wants to be the life of the party, or wants to have fun that night, and an hour later he overdoses—not counting the cost, and, instead, losing his life. That is what happens to those who celebrate this creature's holiday.

As devil worshipers, we considered Halloween to be very special, and we looked forward to celebrating it because we knew the implications and the dark power behind the night. It is very different from every other night in the witchcraft world. It would be like me saying to believers today, How important to you is Good Friday and Resurrection Sunday? Halloween has that much weight and importance to those who dwell on the dark side.

As soon as you make the decision to celebrate this unholy night, you give your allegiance and your identity to the enemy of your soul. Whether consciously or unconsciously, the damage has been done.

I remember the days leading up to Halloween, we devil worshipers had our instructions from the demon world about what had to be done, and we knew it was going to be a long night. I would sleep all day to be rested up and ready for midnight so I could unleash hell on the world into the wee hours of the morning.

Some churches remove the word *Halloween* and call it *Harvest* instead, with members dressing up in costumes, giving out candy and bobbing for apples. It saddens my heart. Turning away from this "holiday" is not missing out on anything, so let us get that off our minds.

If they are trying to use certain secular holidays for evangelistic purposes, to win souls, this is the way I would do it as a minister: I would make it a biblical movie night with popcorn and soft drinks for the kids and grownups, and invite unsaved friends and family. My intention for the event would be to expose the origin and dangers of Halloween, then turn it into a great movie night, with a small teaching afterward from God's Word about His love and the finished work of the cross. Finally, I would have an altar call and make it a special night for all to remember.

The only harvest we should celebrate is the harvest of souls.

For many who celebrate Halloween, that celebration carries over to November 1, which is also known to some as the

Day of the Dead, or All Saints Day, but there is nothing holy about it—it is demonic.

I am surprised at how the world embraces this holiday, because the title of All Saints Day is a deceiving one. We have a picture in our minds that it sounds holy, but there is nothing innocent about it. This holiday is practiced all throughout South and Central America and distant parts of the world, and even in the United States. To the Spanish culture, it is called Día de Muertos, and they celebrate the dead through rituals and ceremonies and even cemetery visits. A good place to go and see for yourselves what this is about would be YouTube. This holiday has nothing holy about it nor anything to do with saints.

In the Bible, when the Lord calls the believers "saints," the term means we have been sanctified by the blood of Jesus Christ and the finished work of the cross. We are set apart for good works to glorify God.

As a minister, I would use All Saints Day to turn the tables on the devil and to celebrate my salvation and the salvation of my family and loved ones. I would use it as an evangelistic opportunity at my church to bring in unsaved people to hear testimonies of God's goodness and how He can transform their lives, too. And that night I would give the devil a black eye in Jesus' name, because many souls would be saved.

The Elephant in the Room

The "elephant in the room" is a metaphor for an obvious truth that is going unaddressed, the problem or risk no one wants to discuss or a "groupthink" that no one wants to challenge.

The uncomfortable yet "obvious truth" about the Church today is that we have become politically correct. We have tolerated the enemy's lies and deceptions and called our churches "seeker friendly" because we do not want to offend anybody. Instead of calling it the Church of Jesus Christ, we have become a club. But Jesus said,

> "Therefore everyone who confesses Me before men, I will also confess him before My Father who is in heaven. But whoever denies Me before men, I will also deny him before My Father who is in heaven.
> "Do not think that I came to bring peace on the earth; I did not come to bring peace, but a sword."
>
> Matthew 10:32–34 NASB

> "He who loves father or mother more than Me is not worthy of Me; and he who loves son or daughter more than Me is not worthy of Me. And he who does not take his cross and follow after Me is not worthy of Me. He who has found his life will lose it, and he who has lost his life for My sake will find it."
>
> Matthew 10:37–39 NASB

We have become delusional and delirious and afraid to lead with the truth of the Lord that will set many free. We have let down our guards. But I come to bring good news with a loving heart. I am willing to be the only one to address the elephant in the room. I would rather you be mad at me than not make it to heaven.

Together, let us regain our spiritual understanding and get back to the cross of Jesus Christ.

I understand there are struggles the Lord Jesus Christ is working out in every church as He moves us from glory to glory. Even in my own personal life I have faced many challenges, and sometimes it has been a roller-coaster ride, but I have learned to live on His Word, His principles and His promises. They have never, ever failed me. And no devil can do anything about that.

Managers of God's House

We have been called to take care of God's house, the Church, in every way. As ministers and leaders, we have neglected and abandoned our responsibility. I thank God not all ministers are guilty of this, but so many are. Let us be honest. We have left our posts and now we are chasing the wind. In other words, chasing the question mark instead of the answer that is Jesus.

There is a remarkable passage in the book of Genesis that describes how Lucifer and the angels neglected and abandoned their posts in heaven.

> And war broke out in heaven: Michael and his angels fought with the dragon; and the dragon and his angels fought, but they did not prevail, nor was a place found for them in heaven any longer. So the great dragon was cast out, that serpent of old, called the Devil and Satan, who deceives the whole world; he was cast to the earth, and his angels were cast out with him.
>
> Revelation 12:7–9 NKJV

A third of the angels chased the question mark, which is Satan, but all along they had the answer, which is Jesus Christ, the Son of God. It is disturbing to say history is repeating itself now in the Church. We are leaving our posts to follow doctrines of demons, clever ideas, false theologies and man-made programs—all catering to the flesh, the things of the world and the devil himself.

Not many have an anguish in their spirit to correct, to confront, to turn back to the place where God wants us to be. Many beautiful believers, because of these consequences, are being destroyed spiritually. Discipleship, baptisms and repentance have become things of the past, and there is a Scripture famine.

My cry for all of us who call ourselves ministers in the unarmed Church is to get back to God, where we need to be. I am sounding the trumpet even for myself: It is time to clean the house of God—sweep it clean of manipulation and witchcraft spirits encountered directly or indirectly.

Satan has unleashed his witchcraft spirits against the end-time Church. He is looking to destroy as many people as he can, and to take us straight to hell with him. And he knows that he has a short time to accomplish this mission. His greatest assignment is to enslave the Church of Jesus Christ. We need to fight back today, not tomorrow, and be consistent and more determined than ever to defeat this fool called the devil.

Let us pray and battle with a holy anger, sending the fire of the Holy Spirit to cleanse and sanctify the pulpits and pews one more time before the Master gets back. We all have to give an account. Are you ready to stand and be counted?

> There shall not be found among you any one that maketh his son or his daughter to pass through the fire, or that useth divination, or an observer of times, or an enchanter, or a witch. Or a charmer, or a consulter with familiar spirits, or a wizard, or a necromancer. For all that do these things are an abomination unto the LORD: and because of these abominations the LORD thy God doth drive them out from before thee.
>
> Deuteronomy 18:10–12

Have no mercy on these spirits. Kick them out.

Prayers of Battle

Repeat these prayers out loud from the mountaintop, mix with faith, and let every demonic force in the spirit realm hear you. As the Church, we must take back our inheritance!

1. Our Lord is a consuming fire. Let the enemies of the Church be consumed.

2. Lord, look at the attacks and release the fire of Your Spirit upon them; we ask You to destroy the spirit of pride in the Church.

3. I speak by the authority and power of the Holy Spirit. Let every witch that infiltrated Your Church from the north, south, east and west be removed in Jesus' name.

4. I frustrate the plans, devices, schemes and wiles of the devil, as well as the plans, devices and schemes of any witches or warlocks that have been assigned to afflict the Church. I uproot them in the name of Jesus.

5. Any witches or warlocks that have infiltrated the Church, be exposed in the name of Jesus now.

6. Any person from the dark side that has been assigned by astral projecting into our church, let the silver cord be cut off in the name of Jesus.

7. I smite with the blood of Jesus seven times any witches that are infiltrating our services and releasing incantations upon the congregation and leaders. Be removed now in the name of Jesus.

8. Any animal sacrifices of any witches against the Church of Jesus Christ, or any demonic altars that have been set up, I destroy them all with the blood of Jesus and the finished work of the cross. I destroy any articles the witches have stolen that represent the Church and its

mission statement, and I smite them with the blood of Jesus, to burn to ashes.

9. Any and all witchcraft planting or burials against the Church of Jesus Christ, I destroy in the name of Jesus.

10. I go into the devil's camp and take back every blessing that he stole from the Church through witchcraft. I take it all back in the name of Jesus.

11. I call upon the Lord to release warring angels from Michael's quarters to dismantle and uproot any witchcraft network in my region. May they be destroyed from the north, south, east and west. I believe this previously mentioned verse in Revelation provides a picture of this type of warfare: "And war broke out in heaven: Michael and his angels fought with the dragon; and the dragon and his angels fought, but they did not prevail, nor was a place found for them in heaven any longer" (Revelation 12:7–8 NKJV). Archangel Michael and the other angels that join with him in the battle are warring angels.

12. I release the ten plagues of Jesus to fall upon every witch, wizard, sorcerer and warlock that is infiltrating the Church of Jesus Christ.

13. For every witch that is chanting, casting spells and astral projecting against the Church of Jesus Christ, I bind every dark work and turn it against your own head until you repent in the name of Jesus.

14. I break and uproot every scheme, pattern and cycle of witchcraft designed to stop the growth of the Church. I destroy them all by the blood of Jesus Christ, in Jesus' name.

15. I release arrows dipped in the blood of Jesus into the enemy's camp to destroy every satanic target that opposes

the Church of Jesus. Let them be destroyed in the name of Jesus.

16. I send confusion into the enemy's camp. I confuse their languages, and let them attack one another, any and all, who are trying to bring down the Church of Jesus Christ.

17. In the name of Jesus Christ, I loose the hands and feet of every believer in the Church to walk out and evangelize.

18. I forbid any witchcraft meetings from taking place here or in any other region where the Church is planted; may the fire of the Holy Spirit fall upon their heads in the name of Jesus.

19. I destroy and curse at the root every witchcraft spell against the Church of Jesus Christ; let it be destroyed, in Jesus' name.

20. I destroy every witchcraft covering and covenant from the first and second heaven and dismantle the operation piece by piece, never to rise up again against the Church of Jesus Christ.

21. I release the bondages of heaven to chase down every witch, warlock, wizard or sorcerer that is standing against the Church of Jesus Christ. I declare this in Jesus' name.

22. May the thunderbolts of Jehovah Nissi strike the head of every snake that has risen up against my church and the Church. I cut off their heads in Jesus' name.

23. Let the path of every devil and every witch assigned against the Church be slippery, and let them spiral out of control to destroy themselves in Jesus' name.

We are the Church of Jesus Christ. We are to take no prisoners in prayer; we are to take back everything that the devil has stolen from us.

When we as believers expose the devil, we weaken him, but when we do not expose him, we empower him. Take that to the bank. When we do not use the weapons of our warfare, then we settle for the mediocre Christian life. Instead, let us rise up as the Church and cause God's enemies to be scattered.

As you continue to turn the pages of this book, you will be equipped to stand as the end-time Church Jesus Christ is coming back for. You will become a spiritual sniper, bringing down targets in the enemy's camp like you have never seen before.

Be a Champion in Christ

God has given us His promise and provision for living a long life: "'Honor your father and mother'—which is the first commandment with a promise—'so that it may go well with you and that you may enjoy long life on the earth'" (Ephesians 6:2–3 NIV). On the other hand, the devil knows that God has made this promise to us. So what does he do? He has unleashed a spirit of premature death to try to cut our days short so that we will die before our time. Today we will stop him in his tracks.

Aggressive Prayers

1. I cancel in the name of Jesus the spirit of premature death that is trying to cut my days short. I destroy his plan and assignment against my life, and I release the Holy Spirit to destroy every blueprint of sickness from the spirit of death in Jesus' name.
2. I come against every spirit of death, cancer, diabetes, heart attack, high blood pressure, suicide and stroke;

I smite you seven times with the blood of Jesus Christ. I abort your plan against my life now in Jesus' name.

3. I declare I shall live and not die and declare the works of the Lord today and forevermore in the name of Jesus.

4. Father, in the name of Your holy Son, Jesus Christ, empower me by the anointing of the Holy Spirit to destroy every demon that has been assigned to monitor my life.

5. I bring destruction now against the devil's camp and the forces of darkness in the name of Jesus.

6. With the sword of the Lord I will chop off the head of every evil spirit the same way David took off the head of Goliath, in Jesus' name. I pluck out the eyes of every evil spirit that is operating through witches, wizards, sorcerers and warlocks that have been assigned to spy on my life. I destroy them all in Jesus' name.

7. I ask God to release blindness into the enemy's camp and cut off every circuit that is trying to infiltrate my purpose and destiny. I bring them down and destroy them completely through the power of the Holy Spirit in Jesus' name.

8. I pray against every satanic hindrance and destroy the strategies that have been planned against me, in the name of Jesus Christ.

9. I hinder and frustrate every assignment of the devil and his demons and whatever methods they are trying to use against me. I burn them down with the fire of the Holy Spirit.

10. I shoot lightning into the devil's camp and upon every demon's head, to confuse and destroy their game plan against my life, in Jesus' name.

11. I bind and rebuke all demonic reinforcements sent by the evil one to attack, hinder or frustrate the plan of God over my life. I dismantle them in the name of Jesus.

12. I confess the sins of my ancestors in the name of Jesus. Lord, I ask forgiveness for the sins of my father's bloodline and the same thing for my mother's bloodline, in the name of Jesus.

13. I renounce and loose myself from every demonic dedication placed upon my life, in Jesus' name.

14. I take authority over all curses that have been spoken over my life, in the name of Jesus.

Lord Jesus, I want to thank You for my victory and Your promises, because through these prayers I stand on the offensive by the power of the Holy Spirit that lives in me and the anointing that You placed upon my life. Today, I am a champion in Jesus Christ, Amen.

I believe in my heart that praying the prayers in this chapter will keep you ahead of any spiritual warfare that may come against you, your family, your loved ones and your church.

Remember, offense in Christ wins championships.

In the next chapter, we will unveil how to beat the devil at his game by knowing his playbook.

Unveiling the Unholy Curtain: No. 21

There are 21 paths or entry points to the most diabolical cults in the dark side. My research shows the number 21 to mean "snake," and the first encounter the Bible records between Satan and humankind is with Eve in the Garden of Eden, where he appears as a snake. You know the story: Satan deceives Eve into disobeying God's command, and she in turn leads her husband into deception and rebellion against God.

Today, there are 21 main false religions that Satan operates to deceive and conquer people from different walks of life, a variety of cultures and diverse ethnic backgrounds. These demonic religions branch out into numerous sub-religions, but they are all intertwined with the kingdom of darkness. If you study them one against another and have what Jesus called "eyes to see" and "ears to hear," you quickly realize—it is a big giant web.

I will give you one example: Santeria, the religion from which the Lord rescued me, means worship of saints. But that definition is a lie. Santeria is the worship of demons. The devil does not play fair, and he delights to deceive—always remember that.

The participants in this occult religion worship the five main gods of Santeria, bringing fruit offerings and water for purity. Now, if you cross over into the Asian community, you find the worship of an Asian deity (demon), and in Asian restaurants, there is a statue in the corner displaying offerings of fruits and water and candles—the same as in the Santeria religion. Two different cultures, but the same demon crossing over and demanding the same kind of worship. This is how the demonic realm entraps innocent people who are looking for the truth, all in the wrong places.

The following is a list of the 21 most common pathways into the dark side:

21 Paths

Palo Mayombe
Spiritualism
Islam
Mormonism
Jehovah's Witnesses
Buddhism
Taoism
Paganism
Shamanism
Catholic worship of saints and obeying human traditions

Shintoism
Santeria
Voodoo
Satanism
Scientology
False Christianity
Hinduism
New Age
Wicca
Kabbalah
Falun Gong

Satan's throne is seated on these religions; they are his bread and butter for reaching humanity because people always look in all the wrong places for something to captivate them. In reality, people are looking for Jesus Christ—even when they do not know it.

The only religion that Satan will never get a grip on is true Christianity because of the finished work of the cross. True Christianity has nothing in common with the other religions, while all other religions have a lot in common with each other because they are owned by one person—the devil. What defines Christianity is a personal relationship with Jesus Christ. God created you to have a relationship with Him.

21 Days of Warfare

The book of Daniel records an amazing account of Daniel receiving his breakthrough after three weeks of fasting and prayer. When he prayed, the Lord heard him on the first day. But it took 21 days of fasting for Daniel to see his blessing come to pass. Even in the 21 days, the Lord had to release an archangel to deal with the prince of Persia—a spiritual principality—before Daniel could receive his blessing. Because Daniel understood spiritual warfare, he fasted and broke through the 21 demonic patterns of the devil's kingdom in the spirit realm. Daniel broke through spiritual bondage and gained his victory.

Look at this amazing story, picking up where the angel speaks directly to Daniel:

> Suddenly, a hand touched me, which made me tremble on my knees and on the palms of my hands. And he said to me, "O Daniel, man greatly beloved, understand the words that

I speak to you, and stand upright, for I have now been sent to you." While he was speaking this word to me, I stood trembling.

Then he said to me, "Do not fear, Daniel, for from the first day that you set your heart to understand, and to humble yourself before your God, your words were heard; and I have come because of your words. But the prince of the kingdom of Persia withstood me twenty-one days; and behold, Michael, one of the chief princes, came to help me, for I had been left alone there with the kings of Persia. Now I have come to make you understand what will happen to your people in the latter days, for the vision refers to many days yet to come."

When he had spoken such words to me, I [Daniel] turned my face toward the ground and became speechless. And suddenly, one having the likeness of the sons of men touched my lips; then I opened my mouth and spoke, saying to him who stood before me, "My lord, because of the vision my sorrows have overwhelmed me, and I have retained no strength. For how can this servant of my lord talk with you, my lord? As for me, no strength remains in me now, nor is any breath left in me."

Then again, the one having the likeness of a man touched me and strengthened me. And he said, "O man greatly beloved, fear not! Peace be to you; be strong, yes, be strong!"

So when he spoke to me I was strengthened, and said, "Let my lord speak, for you have strengthened me."

Then he said, "Do you know why I have come to you? And now I must return to fight with the prince of Persia; and when I have gone forth, indeed the prince of Greece will come. But I will tell you what is noted in the Scripture of Truth. (No one upholds me against these, except Michael your prince.)"

Daniel 10:10–21 NKJV

66

God is good! He cared enough to encourage this godly man with a face-to-face encounter with one of His holy angels. Amazing. Daniel stood strong in spiritual warfare—he was armed and dangerous—and received the victory over the demonic realm. We need to do the same today.

Stop Drinking the Kool-Aid

Satan has a lot of tools and gadgets in his bag of tricks, and these are a few of the most common ones he uses: tarot cards, Ouija boards, tea leaves, palm reading, séances, fortune telling, horoscopes, horror TV shows and movies, demonic video games and books, and the like. Now we also have Satanism afterschool programs, as reported by both Fox News and ABC News. Local Wiccans and other pagan groups offer "family friendly" events and boldly proclaim "children welcome!" You better believe they are welcome. The devil likes to snatch our children when they are young, the same way he got me.

Let me take a moment to put the fortune tellers on notice. This practice has become so common that people think it is all fun and games, but I want to warn the reader about this demonic doorway. First of all, let me state unequivocally that tarot card readers *do not know the future*—only Jesus Christ does. Stop drinking the Kool-Aid and being sucker-punched by lies and deceptions. Are you ready to yank the covers off these phonies? Let me tell you how the game is played on the demonic side. This is how it goes:

When you sit with a medium, he or she will ask you to break the cards into three piles—past, present and future. To impress you, she will tell you all about your past. This will captivate your thoughts. There are familiar spirits at play here, namely demonic spirits that the medium has contracts with.

"Familiar" spirits are those that are simply familiar with you. There are two kinds of spirits in the world today: the Holy Spirit (the Spirit of God) and unholy spirits in service to Satan (demons). During your reading, the demons are reporting back to the witch everything that has taken place in your past.

After the medium is done talking about your past and captivating your mind, she will grab the second deck of cards, which is your present. The same demonic force that knows your past also knows your present. Now those demons are after your heart, your will and your emotions. After the medium is done telling you all about your present life, the demons will have you by the throat because they use fear—that is how the devil works.

And the last set of cards is supposed to be your future, which is hogwash. I played this game for 25 years and made a lot of money at it. Now another demon steps in and starts telling you things that are going to happen in the future; this is called a "setup" in the spirit world. It implants in your mind big question marks: *How could this happen? What will I do?*

At the end of your reading, the fortune teller will say, "You have to do some cleansings and ceremonies to stop these things from happening," and of course, all rituals have a price tag—because it is all about the money. But you leave the witch's house hoping these things will not happen, and you say to her, "I'll get back to you."

What you do not understand is that the demon that was whispering in the medium's ear will go home with you and make all those terrible things happen in your life in a short period of time. So you become desperate and run back to the house of the witch crying out, "Oh wow, you did know the future! Everything you said is happening. I'm ready to do the cleansing ceremony." Now the witch owns your bank account. And the devil has you in his pocket. That was not really your future—just a diabolical setup.

You want to know the *real* future of your life and your destiny? Turn to Jesus Christ.

Remember what the Word of God says:

> For I know the thoughts that I think toward you, says the LORD, thoughts of peace and not of evil, to give you a future and a hope.
>
> Jeremiah 29:11 NKJV

Do not be fooled. Turn to Jesus. Stop chasing the question marks when you already have the answer. His name is Jesus Christ.

Mediums—Agents of the Devil

There is a popular TV program in which the host calls herself a medium, and I believe she lives within the five boroughs of New York City. She captivates her audience by supposedly contacting relatives that have passed away and channeling them through her spirit. She always has messages for individuals in her audience. Let me tell you: What she is doing is a total lie.

The Bible is clear that to be absent from the body is to be present with the Lord (see 2 Corinthians 5:8), and Scripture also declares, "It is appointed for men to die once and after this comes judgment" (Hebrews 9:27 NASB). So to be clear with you, and I say this with a broken heart, many times I myself desired to talk to my dad about certain things when he was alive, and I missed my moments to do so. Maybe there were times when you were angry with a close relative and never had the opportunity to make peace with that person, and then that person suddenly died.

So this medium and her demons, like every other medium, capitalizes on your vulnerability. And the devil seizes the moment, using familiar spirits that will mimic your mom or dad or other relative or close friend that you are trying to communicate with. I played this trick on people for many years, and I can tell you that what you are being told is a total lie.

The evil one can mimic any person to perfection, whether it is with a voice, the same body gestures, a certain fragrance—even re-creating the last conversation you had with that person before they passed on. Remember that you are being set up. Run the other way and do *not* open yourself up. Please, I am warning you: This will affect not only you but eventually your entire family in a negative way.

Satan Loves the Culture

One of the main avenues the devil uses to influence and communicate with humanity is the culture. In the Old Testament Scriptures, God forbade the Israelites to mingle and intermarry with foreign cultures because He knew doing so would lead them away from the true life and purposes they were supposed to have with Him.

We see an example of this as Moses addresses the Israelites he led out of captivity in Egypt en route to the Promised Land:

> "When the LORD your God brings you into the land you are about to enter and occupy, he will clear away many nations ahead of you: the Hittites, Girgashites, Amorites, Canaanites, Perizzites, Hivites, and Jebusites. These seven nations are

greater and more numerous than you. When the LORD your God hands these nations over to you and you conquer them, you must completely destroy them. Make no treaties with them and show them no mercy. You must not intermarry with them. Do not let your daughters and sons marry their sons and daughters, for they will lead your children away from me to worship other gods. Then the anger of the LORD will burn against you, and he will quickly destroy you. This is what you must do. You must break down their pagan altars and shatter their sacred pillars. Cut down their Asherah poles and burn their idols. For you are a holy people, who belong to the LORD your God. Of all the people on earth, the LORD your God has chosen you to be his own special treasure."

Deuteronomy 7:1–6 NLT

In Santeria, spiritualism and Palo Mayombe—which are the three deadliest avenues to the dark side—all the rules are made to seem cultural. *Oh, Santeria is just our cultural tradition*, they may tell you. These religions are from the pits of hell. They control how you dress, dictate the colors you can wear, outline the food you can eat and not eat, declare who you can hang out with or marry and even pit family members against family members. They own you with fear.

In Santeria, when you take part in a ceremony called "Santo," you are to dress in white for 365 days, plus an extra number of days for whatever deity has been assigned to you. I will give you an example. The marine spirit that operates on the rivers is assigned the number 5. So you would dress 365 days plus 5. The religion controls you and brainwashes you for those 370 days.

Even food that you have eaten for many years you can no longer eat, or, you are told, you will die—what a lie! So much deception. The same is true for Palo Mayombe; this

71

occult religion seeks to own the rights to your life until the day you die.

The Spirit of God gives life and liberty; Satan seeks only to kill, steal and destroy—and, in the process, to control you. This is a tragedy. It does not have to end that way for anyone.

Please hear me. I am an ex–devil worshiper, a former general in the devil's kingdom, sounding the trumpet so that you can get out and be set free—both you and your family.

Jezebel: Satan's Dagger against the Church

One of the fiercest and most dominating and controlling spirits unleashed against the Church and God's people is the spirit of Jezebel. Jezebel appears in the Old Testament; her story is told in the books of 1 and 2 Kings. Her name is never mentioned again in the Bible until nine hundred years later in the book of Revelation, spoken by Jesus Christ Himself:

> "But I have this complaint against you. You are permitting that woman—that Jezebel who calls herself a prophet—to lead my servants astray. She teaches them to commit sexual sin and to eat food offered to idols. I gave her time to repent, but she does not want to turn away from her immorality.
>
> "Therefore, I will throw her on a bed of suffering, and those who commit adultery with her will suffer greatly unless they repent and turn away from her evil deeds. I will strike her children dead. Then all the churches will know that I am the one who searches out the thoughts and intentions of every person. And I will give to each of you whatever you deserve."
>
> Revelation 2:20–23 NLT

In the Old Testament, Jezebel lived and walked the earth, but in the New Testament, she represents a wicked spirit. In the Old Testament, Jezebel was the wife of King Ahab, the king of Israel. She was not Jewish. This marriage was actually designed to strengthen Israel's alliance with the Phoenicians. It was all about power and control, but proved to be a disastrous move for Israel.

> And as though it were not enough to follow the sinful example of Jeroboam, he married Jezebel, the daughter of King Ethbaal of the Sidonians, and he began to bow down in worship of Baal.
>
> 1 Kings 16:31 NLT

This devil of a woman was not only controlling, but she had a spirit of murder. That same spirit is alive and well today and is trying its best to destroy every leader that God has called to the Body of Christ.

> Once when Jezebel had tried to kill all the LORD's prophets, Obadiah had hidden 100 of them in two caves. He put fifty prophets in each cave and supplied them with food and water.
>
> 1 Kings 18:4 NLT

Wake up, Church! And take heed of my words. It was Jezebel who had the prophets of God massacred at her command and removed from Israel. She had them exiled and put to death. It is no different today. She is trying her best to destroy the fivefold ministry: apostles, prophets, pastors, teachers and evangelists.

The fivefold ministry represents the voice of God to His Church today. Jezebel is determined by all means possible to silence the voice of God. She rules by control, intimidation and fear. And, as the Church, we must stop playing patty-cake with Jezebel.

Jesus said,

"But I have this complaint against you. You are permitting that woman—that Jezebel who calls herself a prophet—to lead my servants astray. She teaches them to commit sexual sin and to eat food offered to idols."

Revelation 2:20 NLT

Jesus said to His disciples,

"Behold, I am sending you out as sheep in the midst of wolves, so be wise as serpents and innocent as doves."

Matthew 10:16 ESV

Jezebel's MO

The modus operandi of Jezebel's evil spirit is to instill fear in the hearts and minds of God's leaders today, still using the same tactics and weapons that she did in the Old Testament.

Nine hundred years after she first appeared, this same evil spirit has destroyed leaders and mega-ministries. This spirit also is very well known as a destroyer of Christian marriages. The Church needs to rise up and confront this devil head on with the spiritual authority of the Holy Spirit to take back our churches, our ministries and even our families.

Many times, Jezebel works in conjunction with the Ahab spirit. If a church's leadership is strong, she will not go first. The spirit of Ahab is passive, so, often, leaders do not discern its presence. It is as if the lights have been turned out and all the leaders are asleep. At that point, Jezebel goes in for the kill because the only spirit that can tolerate her is Ahab. A setup like this in the Church will need serious spiritual warfare to overcome it.

Another spirit that operates together with Jezebel is the spirit of Delilah, which in the demon world is called "sisters." In this regard, we can consider Samson in the Old Testament to be a metaphor for the Church of Jesus Christ. With strength and anointing, he overtook his enemies until he met Delilah, a seducing spirit. You may know the story: He fell asleep in her lap and she cut off his hair, essentially rendering him powerless.

It grieves my heart that the Church has fallen asleep in the lap of Delilah—much like Samson did—and that we have lost our way and our anointing.

A seducing spirit has captivated many leaders in the Church. Many have bought into a spirit of complacency that has drained the Church's anointing in the same way that Delilah stripped Samson of his anointing. All this happens when we open our doors to the wrong spirit. Our spirit should be opened to only one Spirit: the Holy Spirit.

We need to address the issue of spiritual decline once and for all. It rattles my mind, my heart and my spirit that we find ourselves in this place. I love God's Church, but the truth about our condition must be told. Jezebel is a false prophet. She loves doling out false words and false visions to the Body of Christ. That may sound super-spiritual, my beloved brothers and sisters, but do not be fooled.

Today, many in the Body of Christ call themselves prophets. They give themselves titles of prophet and prophetess, and claim illegal authority, trying to speak over the Body of Christ with no validation or the anointing of the Holy Spirit.

I myself have encountered people who have approached me and said, "I am a prophet of God," and then tried to speak a word into my life. Or a person comes forward with something like: "Thus says the Lord, this is what God is telling me to tell you." These people have been so far off the mark that they could not hit the side of a barn. One person said that God told them I was going to relocate to another country or state. Sometime later, another person who called himself a prophet told me I was going to be pastor and have a great church. On the surface, these words sounded like blessings, but I knew their words were dead because I know my relationship with God and the season I am in and the season He is taking me into. This is why it is so important for every believer to be connected to the Holy Spirit—so you will not fall into any spiritual potholes.

I had to correct these people in love, face-to-face, and pray away what was spoken out of their mouths, in the name of Jesus.

False prophets are inspired by Jezebel herself, poisoning the Body of Christ to weaken believers. I will give you an illustration of a great prophet of my time. The late Pastor Wilkerson was a true prophet, and even he did not dare call himself a prophet. Instead, he called himself a watchman on the wall.

Pastor David did not take God's office lightly. I can prove it to you. In 1973, he wrote an amazing book called *The Vision*. If you were to read it today you might think you were reading the *New York Times* because of all the events he predicted. Many of these events came to fruition. Many times, I have thanked God for Pastor Wilkerson's life and ministry.

In *The Vision*, Pastor Wilkerson mentions that the Lord gave him a prophetic vision of a box—today we know it as a cable TV box—and that many ministers were going to become caught up in pornography through this box. In a 2016 study called *The Porn Phenomenon*, Barna Group found that "most pastors (57%) and youth pastors (64%) admit they have struggled with porn, either currently or in the past. . . . Overall, 21 percent of youth pastors and 14

76

percent of pastors admit they currently struggle with using porn." These wonderful believers are in the battle of a lifetime trying to break away from pornography.

Pastor Wilkerson also prophesied in the book about the collapse of the housing market, in which millions of people lost their homes. He also prophesied regarding the catastrophic tsunami in Japan that took countless lives in 2011.

The End-Time Church

The Church today needs to be armed and ready for the ultimate battle of our lives. Many of us have been hurt and grieved by wonderful leaders who have fallen away because of this one evil spirit. Somehow the spirit of Jezebel made it into their ministry undetected.

We as the Church of Jesus Christ must determine that we are not going to take it anymore. Let us hold our spiritual ground and stand with each other in faith. And the first thing we must do is to stop tolerating Jezebel in our midst. We must kick her out of the Church for good.

In this chapter, you will learn how to recognize the 21 personality traits of a person controlled by the spirit of Jezebel and how she infiltrates the Church. She operates by control, manipulation and intimidation, but there is more to this spirit than those three aspects.

Many times, we fail to identify and discern an attack because we assume that Jezebel only manifests through women. Note that the spirit of Jezebel does not always show up as a female; it can also manifest through a male.

We have lacked the ability to discern in the Spirit the two identities of this demonic force called Jezebel. Because of the times in which we are heading, and knowing that the enemy

77

is alive and well, I believe all church leaders should take the time to teach and equip congregations about how to identify this evil spirit before it takes over their churches. Because if we do not wake up spiritually, this spirit's assignment will destroy leaders and divide and conquer churchgoers, causing unholy division and splits in the Church-at-large. I wonder how many churches could reach their full potential of what God called them to be if they only knew how to deal with this evil spirit.

As I mentioned before, my research shows that the number 21 represents a snake. In the same way Satan used a snake to speak to Eve in the Garden, and also in the New Testament when Paul was bitten by a snake that rose out of the fire, the devil, through Jezebel, is trying to sink fangs into your ministry by unloading false teachings, a false gospel and a fake grace that you can create with delusional and delirious circumstances. You can create a counterfeit Jesus in your mind and believe that you still will make it to heaven. As Paul asked the Galatian church, "Who has bewitched you?" (Galatians 3:1 NKJV).

Today we draw a line in the sand with the blood of Jesus Christ. We are going to fight back in the name of Jesus and the power of the Holy Spirit, knowing and understanding that we have authority over Jezebel, and over Delilah, the seducing spirit, and over the Ahab spirit. Through the power of the Holy Spirit, we will live and not die spiritually.

Jesus taught His disciples that some spirits only come out through fasting and prayer (see Mark 9:29). We need to get back to the principles of the Kingdom of our Lord Jesus Christ by fighting back with the wisdom and the knowledge and the understanding that our Lord Jesus Christ has deposited in us through His Word and through fasting.

78

I would like to share with you the 21 ways that the Jezebel spirit operates in people to destroy your church or ministry. This spirit

1. brings fear (caused Elijah to run);
2. attacks ministers;
3. attacks the anointing and those who are anointed;
4. only does its own will and never God's;
5. gives the appearance of repentance before it attacks;
6. needs to be praised and elevated—it worships itself and gets others to praise it;
7. has a possessive love that destroys and controls;
8. is loyal until you disagree with it—then it rebels against you;
9. does all that is asked of it as long as the request falls into its overall plan;
10. plants seeds of discord in others that often leads to conflict and division in the church;
11. uses others to carry out its evil plan;
12. manipulates others to help them carry out their plans, but works alone;
13. has its own agenda—never God's or others';
14. does not listen to God's voice or anyone else's;
15. is very religious and will say things like, "I heard from God, and He spoke to me," but they do not produce fruit;
16. seeks position in order to control, discredit and reach its goal;
17. is not committed to anyone;
18. seeks affirmation and significance;
19. has illegitimate authority;

20. is a convincing liar;

21. rebels when corrected.

In my spiritual walk, I have learned that the devil does not always show up in full force and all at once. Whether we call them steps, attributes or personality traits, the devil often hides under the spiritual radar, undetected.

I will give you a great example that I learned from a bishop in Dallas who has an incredible ministry. Psalm 91, which demonstrates the power of spiritual warfare, describes the fowler (a metaphor for the devil) and four entrapments he uses as he operates against the believer. I found this particularly fascinating: "The young lion and the serpent you will trample underfoot" (verse 13 ESV).

The young lion is a metaphor for any sin that we think we can control. A bad habit or something we do not surrender may seem insignificant and easy to handle, but whatever we do not kill spiritually by cutting it off at the root will end up killing us spiritually. It would be like having a pit bull puppy, and taking for granted that you can push him around and throw him back into his crate. But what do you do when the dog grows up weighing 75 pounds and has a tremendous bite?

The devil works in the same deceptive way, like the young lion in Psalm 91. Thankfully, God promises protection for those who dwell in the shelter of the Most High! (See verse 1.)

I will give you another great example to be a blessing to you. A man went out to the desert to watch eagles fly. That day, the sky was blue and the sun was out. The man spotted an eagle from a distance and followed it, watching as the eagle swooped down to the ground at 90 miles per hour before taking off again. To his surprise, minutes later, that same eagle dropped from the sky and hit the ground, dead.

The gerbil that the eagle had grabbed to kill and eat ended up killing him. The eagle had not killed the animal right away, as it should have.

Same can be said for the spiritual realm: What we do not kill in the spirit will kill us spiritually.

It is like dying with our purpose and our destiny inside of us because we have allowed the devil and his so-called bride, Jezebel, and every other demonic force, to deal with us when we are supposed to be the ones dealing with them.

Like the Church in the first century of the book of Acts, we need to be armed and dangerous.

Dressing for Battle

Are you dressed for the occasion to take on the devil and his cronies to live on the side of victory? God promised to protect and to uphold your place in the Kingdom, so you must protect what God has entrusted you with.

Are you dressed completely in God's armor? Paul wrote to the church in Ephesus, encouraging them to stay armed and dangerous in their own generation. These are the words of our brother Paul:

> Finally, be strong in the Lord and in the strength of his might. Put on the whole armor of God, that you may be able to stand against the schemes of the devil. For we do not wrestle against flesh and blood, but against the rulers, against the authorities, against the cosmic powers over this present darkness, against the spiritual forces of evil in the heavenly places. Therefore take up the whole armor of God, that you may be able to withstand in the evil day, and having done all, to stand firm. Stand therefore, having fastened on the belt of truth, and having put on the breastplate of righteousness, and, as

81

shoes for your feet, having put on the readiness given by the gospel of peace. In all circumstances take up the shield of faith, with which you can extinguish all the flaming darts of the evil one; and take the helmet of salvation, and the sword of the Spirit, which is the word of God, praying at all times in the Spirit, with all prayer and supplication.

Ephesians 6:10–18 ESV

Every time the Holy Spirit alerts me that some kind of demonic attack is coming my way, I make sure that I am meditating on Ephesians 6, going through the whole chapter to make sure my armor is on right. I believe in my heart that the armor of God represents the Holy Spirit because He is our protector and defender of who we are in Christ.

I strongly advise, as you read through Ephesians 6 and you call out every part of the armor, that you declare it over your life and let the devil know you are putting him on notice that you came to fight in Jesus' name.

Now let us turn our attention to the patterns and cycles of the enemy as he tries to infiltrate our lives and disrupt God's plans for us. Warfare is all about recognizing your opponent's weak spots and premeditating his moves.

Satan uses the same tactics again and again; we humans are prone to falling into his traps so easily. There is nothing original about him. But if you can recognize his patterns, you will see how predictable he is and be that much wiser in your warfare.

Let's roll!

Next, we turn our attention to the battlefield of the mind, because whoever owns the real estate of your thinking has the upper hand in your life. If it is the devil, I urge you to serve him an eviction notice because you cannot serve two masters.

Who Owns the Remote Control of Your Mind?

That is the billion-dollar question the world should ask itself regarding what is going on in society today. No matter our cultural or ethnic backgrounds, who we are, or where we are going, many people today are heading in the wrong direction. It breaks my heart, especially with the younger generation.

So let me ask you again: Who owns the remote control of your mind? In reality, only two people could have their hands on it—Jesus Christ or the devil. Whoever has the remote control in their hands owns the real estate of your mind. If they own that, they own your decisions and where you are heading in your life.

We are in denial as a society. Look around us. Whether you are a believer in Christ or not, look at the poison that has been spilled on the world: the destruction of families, marriages, children; the murders, rapes and abuses of every kind (mental, physical, emotional and spiritual). Look how many people are incarcerated. No one goes to kindergarten thinking they are going to experience such atrocities someday.

On career day, the teacher asks, "What would you like to be when you grow up?" We all raise our hands hoping the teacher will pick us first so we can say with our eyes wide open and a big smile, "I want to be a doctor" or "I want to be a nurse" or "I want to be a firefighter." Little do we know what lies ahead in life and that there is a devil to fight whether we choose to believe it or not.

Sad to say, many Christians do not believe that the devil exists. If you are an unbeliever, you have it twice as worse.

I remember back in the '70s when I was growing up and rap music was taking off. Many nights we would go to the schoolyard where the DJ would connect his turntables to the light pole on the street. It would be a nice summer night, with a light breeze and the sky full of stars. We would go out to the yard to hear the DJ spin the tables, and the emcee would grab the microphone and rap his heart out. We were poor with big dreams. It was a ghetto thing.

There was a song that was played often that spoke about being pushed to the edge until it felt like you were barely able to keep from going under. This could be the theme song of how it feels when the devil owns the remote control of your mind. Only one person in the universe can set you free. It is Christ Jesus, who already won your freedom at the cross. But instead of running toward Him, we think we can find our freedom in the world. We try to find our freedom in going to clubs, drinking, using drugs or hanging out on corners with so-called friends and listening to corrupt music. We think we can go up against the devil on our own.

The devil is like quicksand; he sucks you in a little bit at a time. As you try to pull yourself away with all your strength, he zaps your energy by controlling your mind—and therefore your life. You will never crawl out of the quicksand of your mind. Only God is able to change the channel on your remote control and set you free.

A Cosmic Chess Game

The game of chess is a brilliant game. It is a game of the mind, a game of thinking and a game of strategy. It is also a game of patience and endurance, the ultimate setup in challenging yourself and your opponent to see who is going to outthink the other. The bottom line of chess is to get into the other person's mind and win the game.

As it is in the natural realm, so it is in the spiritual realm. The devil knows how to push the buttons of your mind through repetitive mental conversation loops and damaging words planted in your thought patterns. He enforces these negative patterns so you will obsess on those thoughts. In this way, he can weaken you. He can reconstruct your thinking and create patterns and cycles by opening gateways and portals of your mind, whether you are conscious of it or not, so he can gain access to your mind, will and emotions.

The major tool of the enemy is to have you fantasize and create imaginary situations in your mind so that those ideas can be played out in the physical realm. That is why I do not recommend fantasizing to anyone, because once he has a hold on you those ideas will be played out eventually.

Take suicide. Sometimes we hear about a person who committed suicide, and the first thing we say is that we did not see it coming. The same could be said about a person who is addicted to pornography, who later becomes divorced. Or for anger, bitterness and lack of forgiveness in a person that leads to destruction. As these activities take root in your life, the evil one breaks down your inner man and creates a counterfeit for his convenience to destroy you. For example, if you are a single man, the enemy may point out a woman to you in a way that causes you to fantasize about having a relationship with her. You may start out with good intentions, but the enemy can pervert your intent. Soon you could find yourself caught up in a stronghold of lust. In the kingdom of darkness, this is what we called checkmate.

But I have good news for you. The game does not have to end that way because we can be on offense as believers in Jesus Christ. The greatest example is the finished work of the cross that Christ left us with, totally on offense. He was never on defense. He destroyed the works of darkness on the cross because He was armed and dangerous. Instead of getting hit, He was the one doing the hitting, spiritually speaking.

It is time the Church takes the offensive position, with our quivers full of arrows dipped in the blood of Jesus, shooting into the enemy's camp to destroy every evil target and taking our position of authority seated with Christ Jesus in the highest heaven (see Ephesians 2:6).

In this way, we send confusion into the enemy's camp and change their languages so they cannot communicate with one another. Doing this leads to the shutting down of the first and second heavens where the principalities distribute their orders to the territorial demons in the earth realm. We burn down with the fire of the Holy Spirit their banners and scrolls. The banners represent their position, and the scrolls dictate what assignment they have against us. We are more than conquerors in Christ Jesus.

In this chapter I will teach you how to stand victorious in our Lord Jesus Christ through prayer, and how to take back everything the enemy has stolen from you, your family, your ministry and your life. We are going to show the devil that he picked the wrong Christians to mess with because we are not afraid.

Protecting Your Thoughts

Keep your thoughts out of the devil's hands and safeguard your mind with the prayers I am about to share with you. One of the enemy's favorite tricks is conquering your mind by the words you speak out of your mouth. He has a demon assigned to your speech, to chase after your words.

> Death and life are in the power of the tongue, and those who love it will eat its fruit.
>
> Proverbs 18:21 NASB

To safeguard our Christian walk, we need not only to renew our minds as the Bible speaks about, but also to renew our words and speech. That goes along with renewing our prayer life with a fresh anointing as well as fresh conversations with our Lord Jesus Christ. Protecting our prayer life will keep us three steps ahead of the devil on any given day. I want to encourage and challenge you to step up against the enemy in your life.

God has already given us the victory. We just need to step into it and take it from the devil's hands, the same way God gave the children of Israel the Promised Land but they had to go in there and take it out of the enemy's hand.

There will always be a fight in the spirit realm. It is up to us. How badly do we want our victory? I believe that if you are reading this book you want to be victorious once and for all through the power of the Holy Spirit that lives in you. Now it is time to turn the tables on the devil and position yourself for the victory you are about to receive.

Kick Fear to the Curb

Before we go into the battle you must get rid of all fear, doubt and unbelief. These will hinder your deliverance. The Word of God has principles. Jesus established belief as a principle.

> Therefore I tell you, whatever you ask for in prayer, believe that you have received it, and it will be yours.
>
> Mark 11:24 NIV

Sticking to this principle, we establish the stage against the enemy as we enter the battle for our deliverance. Do not be held back by self-consciousness or embarrassment of any kind because at that point the devil can attack and make you believe that deliverance is not going to happen. I want you to say the following prayer with me out loud, slowly and deliberately from the heart, and give it your undivided attention. If at any moment through this prayer you feel uncertainty, go back and read it again until it sticks in your spirit. Identify yourself with the words of this prayer:

Lord Jesus Christ, I believe that You are the Son of God and the only way to God and that You died on the cross for my sins and rose again from the dead. I give up all my rebellion and all my sins before You. I ask for Your forgiveness, especially for any sins that expose me to any curse. Release me also from the consequences of my ancestors' sins. As a decision of my will, I forgive all who have hurt me, harmed me and betrayed me. Just as I want God to forgive me, I forgive them. I renounce all contracts known and unknown or any occult or satanic agreements. If I have had any contact with occult objects, I commit myself to destroy them. I cancel all of Satan's plans against me, Lord. Jesus, I believe that on the cross You took on Yourself every curse that could ever come upon me. So I ask You now to set me free from every curse over my life in Your name, Jesus Christ. By faith, I now receive my freedom, and I thank You for it.

There is another side to the battle and to making peace with God as you just did. The second part, which many Christians forget to do out loud, is to address the devil and put him in his place by serving him notice that every legal right you have given him over your life, consciously and unconsciously, will be broken today.

So, devil, listen to me. I am attacking you from my position of authority seated with Jesus Christ in the highest heavens at the right hand of God the Father.

And God raised us up with Christ and seated us with him in the heavenly realms in Christ Jesus.

Ephesians 2:6 NIV

That means you are under my feet, along with the wiles and schemes and every fiery dart that you brought upon my life. I destroy you now with the blood of Jesus

89

Christ. I ask God to release angels from Michael's quarters to go on the attack now. I dip arrows in the blood of Jesus Christ and shoot them into the enemy's camp and destroy every target that has my name on it. I break down every demonic altar that has been set up against my family, my loved ones, my ministry and me. I paralyze every demon that has been assigned to me in the season I am in now. I uproot every incantation and spiritual roadblock that the enemy has set against me. I pulverize every attack against me and I curse it at the root, never to return, in the name of Jesus Christ. I void every legal right that the enemy has against my family. I go back ten generations on my father's and mother's sides; be destroyed by the fire of the Holy Spirit. I take back my mind from all tormenting and scorning spirits that have implanted themselves in my mind and thoughts, and I destroy and uproot them with the blood of Jesus Christ and the finished work of the cross. I call back from the north, the south, the east and the west every fragmented piece of my mind—I call them back in the name of Jesus. I speak to my mind to be whole, healed, and delivered out of the enemy's hands, in Jesus' name.

If you believe these prayers in your heart, and you mix them with faith, you will have the mind of Christ.

To get the victory when Satan is trying to steal your life away, you need to understand two things: Our God is great and the devil is limited.

Are you ready to learn how to recognize his old bag of tricks? It starts with destroying patterns and cycles.

Destroying the Patterns and Cycles of the Evil One

But when people keep on sinning, it shows that they belong to the devil, who has been sinning since the beginning. But the Son of God came to destroy the works of the devil.

1 John 3:8 NLT

The satanic world is a world of principles and order—*if* you obey the devil and his principles of the kingdom of darkness, and *if* you obey his rules for your life as you serve him and are committed to him. Outside those boundaries there are no rules and you can do whatever you want to anyone.

When I was in Santeria and Palo Mayombe, we could destroy and take out anyone we wanted to and with no remorse as long as it pleased Satan. I did not deprive myself of anything I wanted. I was driven by the power that I lived on. I saw how the enemy and demons function in this world.

Let me give you an example of what I am talking about. One night around two or three o'clock in the morning, I heard a loud pounding on the terrace door of my apartment, and when I looked out, I saw two burly men. They said they wanted to talk to me. I felt the evil presence upon them, but agreed to meet them in the lobby of the building to discuss what was on their minds.

The men claimed they were the real owners of the apartment and demanded money from me. I responded, "Go take it up with the landlady." I knew these men were heavily into witchcraft, and before they walked away, the last comment that came out of one of their mouths was, "You're going to pay the ultimate price."

A half hour later, I could feel demons bum-rushing the bedroom, trying to destroy me. The demonic forces shook me from my sleep and out of bed. But those two men did not do their homework: They had declared war on the devil's son. Twenty-four hours later, I unleashed hell upon them and the landlady. I summoned demons through rituals of animal blood sacrifices and black candles. When the witchcraft hit them, they never came back—not even the landlady, to collect her rent. I lived in that apartment for nine months rent-free until I decided to move out. That was the power of witchcraft that I had initiated, and that was the price they had to pay.

To me there were no other powers in the universe but the powers of darkness. I thought that was the ultimate power until I crossed over to the other side of the cross, by the blood of the precious Lamb. His name is Jesus Christ. I have no regrets. I live for one person and one person only, the man Christ Jesus.

The Lord has given me the discernment to expose the patterns and cycles of this monster called the devil. There is no power and authority like our Lord and Savior. Take my word for it. I came to tell you and share the good news that Jesus Christ is the ultimate power, and He is all we need.

Exposing the Enemy

Sometimes we unwittingly give the evil one too much credit. Many Christians, even precious brothers and sisters I know personally, fall into the trap of the devil, who works by patterns and cycles because he cannot create anything new. So he uses the same old stuff but dresses it up in different outfits.

This is how the game is played.

One of the most common ways the devil plays the game is through our flesh and the things of the world that control us. Another way may be through so-called friends and ungodly relationships or habits of the past that he clings to, thereby claiming legal rights to keep us in bondage. We are free for a few months and then fall back into what had us bound once before.

For example, if the Lord has delivered you from alcohol, the enemy may set the stage for your downfall by bringing believers who are weak-minded and weak of spirit to infiltrate your life. They befriend you, but little do you know that these brothers and sisters live a casual Christianity. The enemy will capitalize on that to try to drag you back into the mud.

Such believers may believe it is okay to go clubbing and drinking to shake off stress and have a good time, so they try to bring that mess into your own backyard. The devil will use that to bring you back to what God has saved you from—to open that door and take you back into bondage—because temptation, when it is not put in check, is a spiritual killer.

Another pattern may be gossiping or lying. Suppose that you struggled with one or both vices before you were saved. Now the enemy will try to hook you up with Christians who are struggling with the same spiritual weakness. He will make sure they find you, whether in your church or at an event, to befriend you so he can entrap you.

We even see patterns and cycles of the evil one in world events. They show up as headline news in your local newspapers or on the TV, but what appear to be copycat crimes are really the same demonic spirits operating in the spirit realm, moving from one place to another to continue the flow.

This demonic activity is what causes patterns and cycles in our lives if we do not cut it at the root—in our families, our marriages, our ministries and our loved ones. We must be spiritually on guard or these patterns will eat away at us like cancer, causing one tragic event after another.

You even see this in the Church when one pastor is caught in adultery, and a couple of weeks later, another pastor in another region becomes caught up in the same cycle. Or a pastor confesses that he is homosexual, and a short time later, another pastor will declare that he is struggling with the same thing.

We think these patterns are normal but they are not. Pastor Wilkerson used to call these patterns and cycles besetting sin.

Let me describe it another way. Say a precious believer is struggling with pornography. He is free for six months; he is doing well and walking with God, and then the enemy sets a spiritual pothole in his path and he falls in it. Now this saint is like a hamster on a wheel, trying to get off. Back and forth he struggles with the besetting sin. He even sells his laptop to avoid temptation, but then a few months later, he buys another laptop and falls into spiritual repetition. As much as he wants to be free, he finds himself caught in a demonic cycle—a spiritual whirlwind.

This type of activity is demonic to the core, and we need to stop the bleeding through spiritual warfare and by going on the offensive so the Church can be the Church. Let us grab the devil by the horns—enough is enough.

Besetting Sin Is like a Cancer

I would like to share a redemption story that illustrates the power of God over sin—even besetting sin. It has taken me a long time, and with much prayer, to share this amazing story because it involves my second-oldest brother, Julio (his nickname was Jimmy).

I felt compelled in my heart to share his life with you, but before I did so, I called my mother to get her permission to put this beautiful testimony in the book.

My brother lived his life to the fullest. No holds barred. No rules in his life. No morality. At times, I even wondered if he came from another planet. The only thing he and I had in common was witchcraft. Jimmy knew his witchcraft like anyone with a Ph.D. knows his work. He never missed a beat, and he used what he knew against people, and with no remorse.

We attended witchcraft parties together, and did private consulting together, for pay. The only reason I surpassed him in witchcraft was because he took a sabbatical to explore other areas of life. Though he had three kids throughout his lifetime, and even got married at one point, my brother had a taste in his soul for homosexuality.

I remember when it hit home for the first time after his secret was uncovered. My brother fought his demons to please my mother, but his other side did not want to stop partaking of this lifestyle. He would go to gay bars and nightclubs and live that kind of life. In between his partying, he tried to be a parent.

My mother was destroyed and distraught—she wanted to put him out of the house. So Jimmy got his own place, and overnight it turned into Sodom and Gomorrah. He would throw demonic parties that would last for three days: substance abuse, liquor, anything went. People would come in on a Friday night and leave on a Sunday. There was nothing normal about the people who attended his parties. The only rule my brother had at his gatherings was that if you were normal you were not invited. It was a freak show.

But in spite of my brother's mess, I loved him.

As time passed, Jimmy spiraled into the black hole called life with no return. Once in a while he would invite me to go clubbing with him—I always said no. But one weekend he asked me again, and I said, "I'll go with you this time." There was going to be a live show at the club. I thought that meant a live DJ, maybe a Latin singer. Instead, the person who was performing that night was my brother, dressed as a transvestite. As I sat there and bought myself another drink, I wanted to walk out. The embarrassment was so bad; I felt I was being set up. If Jimmy had not been so good at witchcraft himself, I think I would have cast a spell on him that night.

Jimmy's lifestyle went on for years, into his early forties. One funny thing about my family is that the only holiday we celebrated together was Thanksgiving. Somehow, we all ended up at my mother's house. By the time I became a born-again Christian, Thanksgiving was very difficult and crazy at my mom's house. Something about saying "grace" over Thanksgiving dinner stirred up the demons, and Jimmy would jump up from the table and start cursing everything about Jesus. I would shoot him back with the Word of God. Even fistfights broke out because I thought I had to protect Jesus from my brother's filthy mouth.

It came to a head, finally, and when Thanksgiving came around again, my mother declared we would not be allowed to go to her house at the same time. He would go early in the day and I would go later, and vice versa. Eventually my brother took a sabbatical from living a homosexual lifestyle and decided to focus on his marriage. But he still threw his debauched parties. Every time we crossed paths was not pretty. On occasion, when I would see him at my mother's house, he had nothing but filthy things to say about Christianity and Jesus.

One day my brother had a heart attack and ended up in the hospital. As he was being prepped for surgery, the voice of the Lord spoke to me and said, "Go to the hospital and tell Jimmy about Me." The first thing that came out of my mouth was, "Oh no, I'm not going there. He's crazy, and so are his friends by his bedside. Lord, You're setting me up so these people can attack me in the hospital with words and come against me. I'm not going."

I felt a deep conviction in my soul. *Who am I to say no to God?* When I got to my brother's room at the hospital, he yelled from the top of his lungs, "What are you doing here? Get out!"

The Holy Spirit came upon me, and I told him, "Shut up, and look out your window! What's across the street?"

He answered, "Calvary Hospital, a place of death."

97

Jimmy and I both knew that Calvary Hospital was a place doctors sent patients who were in their last days here on earth because there was no more they could do for them.

I told him, "That's where you belong. Count your blessings that you're sitting here on this side of the street, and Jesus has a word for you. No more running. It's time to repent and give God a try."

The Holy Spirit fell in that room. All his friends had left. Only Jimmy and his wife were there. Weeping like a little boy, my brother in his deep sorrow professed the sinner's prayer. His wife wept, too. And minutes later, Jimmy was ushered into surgery.

Days later, Jimmy returned home with joy in his heart. The only priority he had in his mind was to find a church and be baptized, which he did. I attended his baptism and was so proud of him. I recall sitting in the car many times with him, listening to worship music—my brother and I glorifying the King.

One of our favorite songs was "I Can Only Imagine." We played it over and over in the car and worshiped together until we wore out the CD.

Months later, my brother was planning the ultimate setup. He was going to throw his first Christian party and invite all his crazy friends, without them knowing it, so he could minister to them about Jesus. A week before his 45th birthday, he called my mom on a Thursday night to have a good chat. He was going to go over the next morning to help her with her errands. As they ended the phone conversation, he told her that he was grateful for his new lifestyle.

He went to bed that night and closed his eyes, but instead of going to my mother's house that Friday morning, he went to see Jesus. Jimmy went home to the Lord—one week before his birthday.

My brother had planned to introduce Jesus to his friends. It never happened. But God has a way of doing things His way. Days later, I preached at Jimmy's funeral. My mom sat in the front row, broken in a million pieces. And those friends who were supposed to attend my brother's birthday party instead attended his funeral.

I preached my heart out about the redemption story and a man called Jesus. Maybe my brother, when he was alive, never won a soul, but that day at his funeral service, there were homosexuals and transvestites, drug dealers and drug users. And on my brother's behalf, I preached the Gospel for him. What he wanted to do at the birthday party, I did for him at the funeral. Eighteen souls gave their lives to Jesus Christ that day.

God's loving arms were extended for the lost. I know deep in my heart that my brother Jimmy was rejoicing in heaven because his mission was accomplished.

Thank You, Jesus.

Getting Off the Hamster Wheel

There is nothing new about the devil and his attacks. We need to confront him head-on and stop letting the fear that he is all that and a bag of chips paralyze us. One of the first things we should do is be genuine with ourselves, understand the stronghold in our lives, identify it, repent of it, make peace with our Lord Jesus Christ and let it rip against the enemy of our soul.

We must tell the devil to his face that we are cutting ties and legal rights, and burning down with the fire of the Holy Spirit every agreement we have unwittingly made with the devil. Whatever upper hand the enemy has on us, we must renounce. In chapter twelve, you will find spiritual weapons for warfare that you can use in everyday life.

God is ready and able to come to our aid, to send His holy angels to protect us and to fight on our behalf in the heavenly ream.

I love Scripture passages that not only expose the enemy but also show us how God defeats him right in front of our eyes.

Queen Esther faced the devil of her time (Haman) and went on a three-day fast and destroyed him; through her consecration, boldness and prayer, God gave her and her people the victory.

If we go a little further, in the book of Daniel, we read about the three young men, Shadrach, Meshach and Abednego, who were among the Jewish captives in Babylon. The devil put a death sentence on their lives, but God had the last word. They refused to bow down to a statue of the Babylonian king, declaring that they would only worship the one true God. Even a fiery furnace could not consume them because a fourth Man showed up in the furnace—the pre-incarnate Christ—and kept the fire from destroying their lives.

These three young men told the evil king, "King, do whatever you want with us because we know our God saves, and we bow down only to Him."

Even the beloved Daniel was thrown into a lion's den because some devils showed up and accused him about his prayer life. But our God shut the mouths of the lions, and nothing happened to Daniel.

In the New Testament, when Peter was put in jail and the devil put him on death row to be executed the next day, God dispatched an angel to set him free.

My beloved brothers and sisters, what the devil meant for evil in our lives, God will turn around for our good, and He will get glory out of every fiery dart the enemy throws our way. God is the same yesterday, today and forever.

Prayer: The Devil's Kryptonite

I know a precious pastor named Sandra Sarraga. She and her husband, Alex, are my spiritual covering and they live in Orlando, Florida. They have a wonderful church called Champions Ministries. In her younger years as a believer, Sandra was in the demonic attack of her life in the middle of the night, and she jumped out of her bed and ran into her living room. That night her husband was not home; he was a flight attendant. As she jumped into spiritual warfare prayer she saw a dragon with an object in its mouth and blood squirting out. She started to pray fearlessly. That night she did not go to sleep, but in the morning, she went to work as normal. When she got to work, people wore serious looks, and she asked someone, "What's wrong with everybody? They have a strange look on their faces."

Her coworker said, "You didn't hear the news this morning?"

Sandra shook her head. "What news?"

"Pan Am flight 103 was blown out of the sky," her coworker answered. "Everyone on that flight passed away."

Alex was a flight attendant for Pan Am. He had been assigned to another flight, but because flight 103 was short one flight attendant, he was asked to move. Alex went onto flight 103 and started to prepare, when at the last minute, the flight attendant who originally had been assigned to that flight showed up, and he was sent back to his other plane.

Alex was spared because his wife decided to get up and pray. At the time, Sandra did not have full disclosure for why she was praying or for whom she was praying. She was simply obedient to the Holy Spirit anyway. When God puts someone in your heart, do not wait until later to pray. Pray at that very moment. Your prayers could save someone's life from a demonic attack.

This is a good lesson, because there have been many times in my Christian walk when God woke me up at two or three o'clock in the morning from a dead sleep to pray. Sometimes, because we are so tired, or maybe lazy, we choose not to get up. Big mistake. Never get comfortable in your prayer life. Be up and ready like a good soldier of Jesus Christ.

It has been an amazing journey through this thing called life, holding the hand of Jesus and with my other hand touching people's lives. To God be the glory forever. Amen. Only He can do this.

In 1997, I had an epiphany that my father was never a good dad to my brothers and me. So I decided to take a sabbatical from witchcraft because I knew that I was not being a good dad to my daughter. I wanted to change that in my life, but the devil was not happy about it. I did not care what the devil had to say; I was going to do it anyway. And sometime later, after I was disobedient to the dark side, the devil struck my eyesight and left me completely blind. It was such a demonic attack that neither doctors nor specialists could explain how it happened. I was completely blind for one year, and I registered with the New York State Commission for the Blind.

It is one thing to be born blind and never see, and another to grow up seeing and then become blind. That is a lot more to suffer, I believe. In my blindness, I still took my sabbatical from witchcraft, but I did not see my daughter for one year because I did not want her to see me in my condition.

Through seven surgeries, and after returning to witchcraft, my eyesight was completely restored. Two years later

I became a born-again Christian because of the grace of God—He did not forget me. He came and rescued me. But in 2002, after being a believer for a few years and growing in the Lord, the devil showed up again and sucker-punched me spiritually. He took away my eyesight for three-and-a-half months.

I was floored. He kept taunting me, saying, "Where is your God now? Look at you. You look like nothing; you're worse than nothing." I was stunned and down for the count for those months. I could not believe that history had repeated itself. But somehow as a young believer I knew that God would give me the victory.

On Good Friday, I went into a four-hour eye surgery. When I came out of the operating room, the doctor told me I needed to go home and lie down so my eyes could recover. Instead, that evening I stepped into my church blind, to worship God. Because no matter the outcome of my situation, I still knew that He had things under control, and I was not going to let the devil get the last laugh. I was going to go down fighting and trusting my Jesus.

And guess what? God never fails. Three months–plus later, I had 20/25 vision, and the doctors could not explain scientifically how that happened. These were amazing doctors who were Jewish, but not believers, and each in their own way said, "There's someone in heaven that loves you."

My response to them was always, "The one in heaven has a name: His name is King Jesus."

So what I want to convey to every person who reads this book is to never give up. Today, you can earn your Ph.D. in spiritual warfare.

Get Your Ph.D. in Spiritual Warfare

In the history of our personal education, many of us strive for perfection. We try our best to study, to show ourselves approved, to get the best grades in school and the highest GPAs in college. We study hard; we cut back on things in our life that are distractions so we can chase after the highest level of education. Whether we are pursuing a bachelor's degree, a master's degree or a Ph.D., many of us give up whatever is distracting us and holding us back from reaching our education goals. Some of us even try our best to get into an Ivy League school.

As we do this in the natural, now as believers we need to step into the supernatural and get our Ph.D. in spiritual warfare. No more playing games, and no more compromising with the enemy of our soul. It is time to win.

The Bible says we have the mind of Christ:

"Who has known the mind of the Lord so as to instruct him?" But we have the mind of Christ.

1 Corinthians 2:16 NIV

From this Scripture we have a promise of our Ph.D., having the mind of our Lord and Savior—a winning mind, not a defeated one. Please understand. The fight must be won inside your heart and mind, beating the devil and his gang, before you even step onto the battlefield. You must know in your heart that you have already received the victory because it is not what you see in the natural that is actually right in front of you—it is what is happening in the supernatural. And you can only see this if you have the mind of Christ.

The Story of You, the Story of Me

Let me ask you a sincere question: How important is your relationship with God? How important is your walk? Know this one thing, that God has a book about you and one about me. He wrote something about you in heaven. I will even go as far as to say that God has a library in heaven, and His library is full of books. Even Jesus wrote a book about Himself: the Bible.

One of the most tragic things that can happen to you and me, or to one of those books in God's library, is that it will sit on the shelf collecting dust and never be read. Do not let your life end up that way in God's library.

It would be like a mother dying with her baby still inside her. What a tragedy.

We were born in the Spirit for spiritual warfare. Do not settle for a high school diploma or an associate's degree—or even a bachelor's degree. There is nothing wrong with those pursuits, but let us stretch ourselves and go beyond our comfort zones to obtain a Ph.D. in spiritual warfare. Let it be the saddest day, not for you and me, but for the devil, because he will not be able to stand a chance against the fight you will bring to him, through victory in Jesus Christ.

We need to know our God-given authority, find our rhythm in the fight and take back what the enemy has stolen from us, those things God has entrusted to us. It requires putting our foot on the devil's neck once and for all.

There is even a biblical precedent for this:

> And it came to pass, when they brought out those kings unto Joshua, that Joshua called for all the men of Israel and said unto the captains of the men of war which went with him. Come near, put your feet upon the neck of these kings. And they came near, and put their feet upon the necks of them.
>
> Joshua 10:24

We must not give the devil an inch in the fight because he will take a foot. Later he will take a yard. So we need to stand on God's promises. I will share this Scripture promise with you:

> For though we walk in the flesh, we do not war after the flesh. (For the weapons of our warfare are not carnal, but mighty through God to the pulling down of strong holds.)
>
> 2 Corinthians 10:3–4

Getting your Ph.D. in spiritual warfare is not something that happens overnight, but by taking the right spiritual steps you will be on your way. Let us strengthen our position in the spiritual fight. Declare these prayer points with me:

1. I confess in the name of Jesus that I am a child of God. I declare and decree that I am born again by the Holy Spirit. I know that it is true that Jesus Christ became a curse for me.
2. I am the righteousness of God through Christ Jesus. I am a citizen in God's Kingdom through Jesus Christ and the finished work of the cross.
3. I am the head and not the tail (see Deuteronomy 28:13). I am above and not beneath. I can do all things through Christ Jesus, who gives me the strength (see Philippians 4:13).
4. Greater is He that lives in me than he who lives in the world (see 1 John 4:4). My body is the temple of the Holy Spirit (see 1 Corinthians 6:19).
5. I am blessed with all spiritual blessings in Christ Jesus.
6. Before I was formed in my mother's womb, God already had a plan for me. I am not a mistake (see Psalm 139:13–16).
7. Satan, I remind you that the finished work of the cross of Jesus Christ has destroyed you, and you are a defeated foe.

These are the arrows in our quiver, dipped in the blood of Jesus, ready to shoot into the enemy's camp to destroy every evil assignment against you and me.

Declare this out loud:

Today, no weapon formed against me shall prosper.
Every demonic tongue that speaks against my life, let it

be condemned now in the name of Jesus. By the power in the name of Jesus Christ, I quench every satanic fiery dart turned against me.

Never Let Down Your Guard

We need to know as servants of the Lord Jesus Christ that the higher we go, the more we will encounter "new levels and new devils," as the saying goes. Never get comfortable in your own spiritual skin. Understand that at any given moment the spiritual channel can be changed, and we must be ready to position ourselves against every demonic attack that is trying to throw us off guard. We need to discern and be spiritually alert at all times.

There is no time for spiritual laziness. When that happens, casualties result—and this should never be. When Jesus Christ made Himself known to the world, when He called from the cross, "It is finished," He meant that He had equipped us with every spiritual blessing we would ever need in this life and in the life to come.

Paul made this clear:

Ever since I first heard of your strong faith in the Lord Jesus and your love for God's people everywhere, I have not stopped thanking God for you. I pray for you constantly, asking God, the glorious Father of our Lord Jesus Christ, to give you spiritual wisdom and insight so that you might grow in your knowledge of God. I pray that your hearts will be flooded with light so that you can understand the confident hope he has given those he called—his holy people who are his rich and glorious inheritance.

I also pray that you will understand the incredible greatness of God's power for us who believe him. This is the same mighty power that raised Christ from the dead and seated him in the place of honor at God's right hand in the heavenly realms. Now he is far above any ruler or authority or power or leader of anything else—not only in this world but also in the one to come. God has put all things under the authority of Christ and has made him head over all things for the benefit of the church.

Ephesians 1:15–22 NLT

So strike the devil in front of you and knock him to the foot of the cross. Stop fighting your fight with a warfare GED—our Lord Jesus Christ has equipped us with a Ph.D. in spiritual warfare. The Bible makes it clear that we are seated in the highest of heavens with Jesus Christ. That is where we fight from.

Stop fighting the devil and his cronies from where he is, in his low position, because he is not higher than our Lord Jesus Christ. There is victory yesterday, today, tomorrow and forevermore. Do not let the devil play you and draw you into his game. The devil's education is no higher than a GED.

Jesus declared to our brother Peter a statement so powerful that it shook the gates of hell and blew the doors wide open. He said, "Upon this rock I will build my church; and the gates of hell shall not prevail against it" (Matthew 16:18). The last time I checked, I *am* the Church of Jesus Christ. So, devil, get out of my way or get run over, in Jesus' name.

Let us no longer be stagnant, seeker friendly and politically correct. None of these will chase the devil away. Many of us, sad to say, believe in the phony theology that if we do not mess with the devil, he will not mess with us. Really? Are we for real? Are we kidding ourselves?

The devil does not *play* at being the devil—he *is* the devil. The Word of the Lord says this:

Be sober, be vigilant; because your adversary the devil, as a roaring lion, walketh about, seeking whom he may devour.

1 Peter 5:8

Do not make it easy for the devil by giving him so much credit when he is a defeated foe. I remember when I was living on the other side of the cross how I used to live dangerously (spiritually), and in all of my battles I did not let the other person breathe or take a time-out or go on vacation. I worked consistently to get my victory. I pushed back in demonic spiritual warfare.

How much more should I push back today, now that I am on the other side of the cross, knowing that my Jesus Christ has won the victory and handed me the keys to the Kingdom? He has made me a victor in spiritual warfare, and He has done this same thing for you.

It is funny that when we were nonbelievers in the world, we did not back down from anyone or anything. We were scrappers, ready for a fight. Now that we are believers, we treat everything on the dark side that opposes us with white gloves. That is crazy. Trust me, my beloved brothers and sisters, the devil does *not* wear white gloves. He has a spiritual sledgehammer, and he wants to pound on us like we are piñatas.

I tell you today, you have to take the white gloves off and get into the fight against the enemy of your soul, turning the tables on him through the power, fire and Shekinah glory (divine presence) of our Lord Jesus Christ. Let everything burn to ashes in the kingdom of darkness forevermore in Christ Jesus. Fear not; we as the Church of Jesus Christ will not be moved. We have seen too much in Jesus to doubt now.

Be ready, even when you think you have a day off from the battlefield.

I Am Still Standing, Devil

As soon as I was converted from darkness to light in my new Christian life, I thought I had left the demonic world behind for good, never to look back again.

But the devil came looking for me when I was not looking for him. Do not be dismayed if the same thing happens to you—it means you are a threat to his kingdom.

One night I went to bed just like normal. Deep into the hours of the night, I felt someone come into the room. My doors and windows were closed, and I lived by myself; no one else had keys to my place. As I heard footsteps in the room, I knew right away that something was not normal. An eerie feeling overtook my apartment and the room went ice cold. Clearly, I was dealing with something not from this world. The presence moved around my bed, the footsteps continuing, but they did not sound like a normal person's.

The demonic spirit decided to sit down on the side of my bed, and from the top of my head to the soles of my feet my body went cold. All my hairs stood up on end. The spirit lay on my body, trying to see if I would turn toward it, but I froze, as if in a state of shock. The only thing that came to my mind in that moment was to pray the best way I knew how.

As a young believer, I did not have a prayer life. All I did was put words together that I heard from other members of the church. I tried to pray like they did. The spiritual channels in this thing that was on my bed changed as I kept praying. It grabbed me by the throat and lifted me off the bed. That night I thought I was going to die. I started to pray faster, rambling words along with the name of Jesus. The faster I prayed, the more the demonic spirit shook me in a violent

112

way. As I repeated the name of Jesus, it finally released me and I fell back onto the bed. My bed started to shake until the spirit left the room. And then everything in the room shifted back to normal. I stayed up for the rest of the night, just in case the demonic spirit came back.

For the first thirty days of my Christian walk, different demons came into my home every other night to torment me, to catch me off guard as I tried to get some sleep. I tried my best to sleep during the day so that at night I would be prepared for the encounter and be able to fight back the best way I knew how in prayer.

If I had known then what I know now about spiritual warfare, it would have been a different fight. I did not understand that spiritual warfare was alive and real. The Church needs to catch up with the program that Christians do get attacked and that they must be ready for battle. I learned this firsthand in those early days of my Christian walk.

We must be armed and dangerous. If you find yourself a victim of night terror attacks, know that you are not alone. Learn that when you get spiritually sucker-punched in this kind of fight, you must get back up quickly, shake off the fear and go into spiritual warfare mode.

Today, here is what I would do. I would identify the attack and paralyze the demon through spiritual warfare prayer, putting him on notice that I am fighting him from my position of authority seated with Jesus Christ. The demon will understand that he is entering into a fight that he has already lost. I would smite this demon and weaken his power through the blood of Jesus Christ, so that he has to leave.

That is how I fight today. The Bible says we have to be ready in season and out of season (see 2 Timothy 4:2).

Facing the Devil on Fifth Avenue

Even during the day, the devil will come at you. It happened to me with a warlock from my past.

One weekday afternoon, as I was walking across Fifth Avenue at 57th Street in New York, minding my business and rejoicing in Jesus about how good He had been to me, right there in front of my eyes was an ex–cult member I had not seen in the several years since I had become a Christian. He was fourth in rank in the occult. I waited patiently as he crossed the avenue and came up to greet me.

"Hello, John, how are you?" he said, his dark eyes trying to pierce through me. "Long time no see," he added, knowing full well that I was a Christian and, to him, a traitor marked for death. This was his golden opportunity to strike me spiritually.

He stretched out his hand, and as we made contact it felt as if everything on Fifth and 57th went into slow motion. He refused to let go of my hand, and I wondered what was happening as he held it in his firm grip. He locked eyes with me, unblinking, so I broke the grip of the handshake. When our hands broke apart, everything went back to normal, at its usual pace. We stood there confronting each other, spiritually, physically, mentally and emotionally, and he started to shake like he was going into convulsions. I wondered what was going on. Since I had not seen him in years, maybe, I thought, he had Parkinson's disease, but I soon realized he was being demon-possessed at two o'clock in the afternoon in the middle of Fifth Avenue. As he tried to speak to me, his eyes rolled back in his head. All I saw were the whites of his eyes. He could not control himself and did not know what was happening, like some force hit him straight on and knocked away all his powers. As he backed away from me, we said our good-byes. I continued down the sidewalk, and the Holy Spirit clearly said to me, "He was trying to curse you, and I broke the curse." I praised and thanked my Lord Jesus Christ for loving me and protecting me.

He had been sent by the enemy to catch me off guard during the day. The devil can bring the fight to you at any given time. We need to discern and be prepared and quick on our spiritual feet, so that we can overcome any adversity or any fiery dart of the enemy.

I have learned through Jesus Christ how to fight back in a new spiritual way—armed and dangerous.

There is a great example in the book of Acts about how demonic attacks come in different disguises. One such attack that the apostle Paul experienced happened when he and Silas were out doing the work of the Lord, preaching the good news of the Gospel. But in the crowd, there was a young girl bound by a demon, yelling out daily, "These men are servants of the Most High God, who proclaim to you the way of salvation" (Acts 16:17 ESV). Paul discerned through the Holy Spirit that this young woman was bound by a demon, or a deceptive spirit, and he cast it out in the name of Jesus.

Thankfully, the apostle Paul discerned this evil spirit, because its assignment, through the servant girl, was to entrap the people after Paul and Silas left the region. If Paul had stayed quiet, the people would have believed the slave girl was in alignment with Paul and Silas's message, and she would have continued her witchcraft.

We need to examine this illustration very carefully and for the sake of our Christian walk, not brush it off. On the surface, the girl's proclamation may have looked godly and very commendable. But far from it—the girl's daily announcements were actually stirring up dissent. We need to pay close attention when we have a check in our spirit that the Holy Spirit is trying to tell us something. Otherwise, our tendency would be to miss it. A good lesson for all of us today.

Are you ready to enter into the promised land of your life, your destiny and your purposes with the Lord Jesus Christ? We have been promoted through the finished work of the cross to sit at the right hand of God through His Son, Jesus Christ. He is our Ph.D. in spiritual warfare! Thank You, Jesus, for giving us our degree and that every battle has been won through faith in You.

Say these prayers with me:

- I declare and decree that I cannot fail.
- I declare and decree that I turn back every negative arrow that is against me and send it to the enemy's camp, in Jesus' name.
- I declare and decree that I am an overcomer in Christ Jesus.
- I declare and decree that I am triumphant in every season of my life, in Jesus' name.
- I declare and decree today, not tomorrow, that no weapon formed against me shall prosper, but only the Lord's plans for my life will prosper, in Jesus' name.
- I quench every fiery dart of the enemy against me today, in the name of Jesus.
- Today I am victorious and an overcomer because greater is He that lives in me than he that lives in the world. Thank You, Jesus.

Know this one thing: Having a Ph.D. in spiritual warfare is not only about waging a good fight against the enemy, but maintaining that stance through a relationship with the Holy Spirit, who is our best friend and wants victory for all who put their trust in Jesus Christ.

Fighting Back with Our God-Given Authority in Jesus

As the Church of Jesus Christ, which He left on the earth to represent His name, we are empowered to take down demonic strongholds, defeat the devil's game plan and go into the devil's territory without fear and wreak havoc. We do all this by our God-given authority that Jesus won for us at the cross.

Too often we allow unbelievers to dictate to us how we should live. We even allow the craftiness of the world to creep into the Church and weaken our relationship with the Lord, watering down our call and the responsibility God left us. The devil has used pressures to weaken our God-given authority, beating us down spiritually to the point of compromise—making us believe that we have lost our way. Ultimately, we risk distorting God's character.

Satan is clever. If he can make us believe that God is sick and tired of us, that He does not love us or has given up on us, then we have nowhere to turn and repent—and the devil wins the fight. This is the oldest trick in the enemy's playbook; do not buy into it.

Many believers today cannot even rebuke or bind up or cast out evil spirits of any kind. Without knowing who you are in Christ and understanding your God-given authority in Him, you have no authority. And you certainly have no fight. As the Church, we have become a social club, and it breaks my heart. I am sure it grieves God's heart even more.

The Bible illustrates what happens when a person tries to fight the forces of evil without legitimate God-given authority. Read this account found in Acts:

> Now God worked unusual miracles by the hands of Paul, so that even handkerchiefs or aprons were brought from his body to the sick, and the diseases left them and the evil spirits went out of them. Then some of the itinerant Jewish exorcists took it upon themselves to call the name of the Lord Jesus over those who had evil spirits, saying, "We exorcise you by the Jesus whom Paul preaches." Also there were seven sons of Sceva, a Jewish chief priest, who did so.
>
> And the evil spirit answered and said, "Jesus I know, and Paul I know; but who are you?"
>
> Then the man in whom the evil spirit was leaped on them, overpowered them, and prevailed against them, so that they fled out of that house naked and wounded. This became known both to all Jews and Greeks dwelling in Ephesus; and fear fell on them all, and the name of the Lord Jesus was magnified. And many who had believed came confessing and telling their deeds. Also, many of those who had practiced magic brought their books together and burned them in the sight of all.
>
> Acts 19:11–19 NKJV

These men had a false authority, all because they went to church (synagogue) and their father was a high priest (which is like a pastor), but they had no personal relationship with Jesus the Messiah. That day, the demon made the ultimate statement: "Jesus I know, and Paul I know, but who are you?"

Even the demon understood the principle of Jesus Christ's authority in us. And when the demon looked at the seven sons of Sceva, he saw nothing in them—and they got the most amazing beat down. They even lost their socks. We know that the beating was so good that they had to go clothes-shopping after that. Shame on them.

The Greatest Fight in the Wilderness

As soon as Jesus came up out of the cold waters of baptism, He was armed and dangerous, and the Holy Spirit led Him into the wilderness.

> Then Jesus, being filled with the Holy Spirit, returned from the Jordan and was led by the Spirit into the wilderness, being tempted for forty days by the devil. And in those days He ate nothing, and afterward, when they had ended, He was hungry.
>
> And the devil said to Him, "If You are the Son of God, command this stone to become bread."
>
> But Jesus answered him, saying, "It is written, 'Man shall not live by bread alone, but by every word of God.'"
>
> Then the devil, taking Him up on a high mountain, showed Him all the kingdoms of the world in a moment of time. And the devil said to Him, "All this authority I will give You, and their glory; for this has been delivered to me, and I give it to whomever I wish. Therefore, if You will worship before me, all will be Yours."

121

And Jesus answered and said to him, "Get behind Me, Satan! For it is written, 'You shall worship the Lord your God, and Him only you shall serve.'"

Then he brought Him to Jerusalem, set Him on the pinnacle of the temple, and said to Him, "If You are the Son of God, throw Yourself down from here. For it is written:

'He shall give His angels charge over you, to keep you,' and, 'In their hands they shall bear you up, lest you dash your foot against a stone.'"

And Jesus answered and said to him, "It has been said, 'You shall not tempt the Lord your God.'"

Now when the devil had ended every temptation, he departed from Him until an opportune time.

Luke 4:1–13 NKJV

In this illustration, my amazing Jesus was not a pushover or a softie. I think of what He did like this: It is like giving someone a head start, letting him run for about ten blocks, making him think that he is winning the race, but suddenly, when you pass him by, all he sees is the back of your head. And he is completely dumbfounded. How did that happen?

In other words, you are in a drag race and you let the car beside you take off. The other driver thinks he is winning the race—he could even bet his life on it. When he looks in the rearview mirror, he does not even see you. Then you blow right by him so fast that the paint job on his car falls off.

That is what Jesus did to the devil in the wilderness.

Jesus fasted for forty days, weakening His human body, and then allowed the devil to show up to give Him three of his best shots. When the devil was done, Jesus ripped out His sword, which is the sword of the Spirit—the Word of God—and sliced and diced the devil like a cucumber.

What an amazing, awesome and powerful example Jesus left us. On that Scripture in Luke alone, we should bet our lives. And I say this boldly: Instead of the devil looking for us, we should be looking for him. It is time to live outside of the box, outside of the borders, and be radical for Jesus Christ.

There is no reason to fake it when the Lord Jesus Christ has made it easy for us to have the real, genuine authority in Him.

As I write this chapter, I have been prompted by the Holy Spirit to never forget to teach the children and young people in the Kingdom how to war in the Spirit. And that is where we turn our attention first in the next section.

Take a Warrior Stance

As believers, we are enlisted in the army of the Lord. We must exercise this power (our spiritual muscle) through the Holy Spirit that God has given us. We should give the devil something to think twice about when he tries to trespass into our spiritual territory, against our families, against our ministries, against our marriages, against our finances, against our health, against our homes and against our children. We are equipped to cage up these devils once and for all, never to return, and to set the judgment of God upon their heads and ask God to release holy angels to fight on our behalf.

Say these prayers with me and mix them with faith:

Father, I pick up the weapons of my warfare. By the blood of Jesus Christ, I stand in the devil's face in this battle. I pray to the Lord to release warring angels to come down and fight on my behalf in Jesus' name.

I break every demonic altar that has been set up against my family and me in the spirit realm by fire; I destroy them in the name of Jesus Christ. I destroy all powers of the dark side that are working against me, my family and my ministry.

I rebuke and bind every astral projecting person who is trying to infiltrate my home, in the name of Jesus. I cut off every assignment of the devil and his demons that is trying to destroy my marriage, in the name of Jesus.

I send Holy Ghost fire upon every devil in the enemy's camp and destroy every spirit of infirmity that is attacking my body, in the name of Jesus. I break down and dismantle every satanic altar that has my picture or my clothing or my hair—I smash them down now with the blood of Jesus Christ.

Father, I take back in the name of Jesus everything that the cankerworm and the locust have eaten from my life and my loved ones' lives, in Jesus' name. I pour fire upon every devil's head and every unclean spirit and every witch that has risen up against my family, my spouse, my children, my finances, my church and me. I smite them with the blood of Jesus seven times and destroy them, never to rise again, in Jesus' name.

I seal my family, my ministry and my church in the blood of Jesus Christ and declare a wall of fire around them (see Zechariah 2:5). The same wall of fire that God put on Job, I put on my family, my spouse, myself, my ministry, my church and my calling.

124

I love my brothers and sisters in the Lord. After 25 years of life in the enemy's camp, I want to be a blessing to the Body of Christ and teach you through the Holy Spirit that the enemy does not stand a chance against us. And I want all believers to know that whatever life you have left here on earth, and whatever years are allotted to you, may they be the best years of your life in Christ Jesus, because God does not make junk. He makes precious people like you and me.

Remember this: Fight back. Take your stand. Be the best Christian you can ever be, and make Jesus Christ proud.

The whole message of *Armed and Dangerous* is to help believers understand their God-given authority and to put the evil one on notice that we are not going to lose the fight or our place. It cost Jesus everything for us to stand here in God's Kingdom, which is a place of honor. You can bet that after you are done reading this chapter, the world, the devil and your flesh will not move you from this place of authority ever again.

Once you learn to be armed and dangerous, and to stand your ground, you can take back lost territory.

10

How to Take Back Lost Turf

When I was a little boy growing up in the South Bronx of the '70s, when street gangs ruled our neighborhoods, there was no area that you could walk into and not encounter a street gang. It was all about who was the biggest, who was the baddest and, in the end, who controlled or owned more turf.

My neighborhood was a jungle. In those days, it was safer to live in the Bronx Zoo with the animals than to live on the cold streets of the South Bronx. You could touch the violence in the atmosphere. It was evil to the core, all because people wanted respect for their turf.

At any moment while I was walking to and from school, a rival gang could show up on neighborhood turf, sparking a shootout or stabbing. We would run behind parked cars or sometimes even duck under the cars so the spraying of the bullets would not get us. As a child, with my heart beating at ninety miles per hour, I would run fast, hoping I could make it home to my doorstep.

I never understood why so much rage and violence could take place at any given time. Later as a young boy, I became friendly with the neighborhood gang and asked the ultimate question: Why so much violence in the streets? They responded, "Hey man, get with the program, dude. We're fighting for our turf and protecting our turf. We can't let those punks come in here and take over our turf, even if we have to die for it."

As it is in the natural, so it is in the spiritual. As believers in Jesus Christ, we are fighting with supernatural weapons. We are guarding our salvation, our purpose and our destiny because the enemy of our soul is tenacious and ready to fight. The good news is that the story does not have to end that way because if you read a little further, you see that Jesus came to give us life and life more abundantly.

> The thief does not come except to steal, and to kill, and to destroy. I have come that they may have life, and that they may have it more abundantly.
>
> John 10:10 NKJV

In order to take back the turf the enemy has stolen from us, we must first understand and believe with all our hearts that Jesus came to destroy the works of the evil one (see 1 John 3:8).

That is the last nail we will use in the coffin. If we will stand on this principle we will get back our lost turf from the enemy's camp. The blood of Jesus Christ is all-powerful to break and release the enemy's grip, to recover it all.

Setting the Stage to Recover Your Turf

To be victorious in the fight we must be filled with the power of the Holy Spirit. The Word of the Lord says, "Not by might nor by power, but by My Spirit" (Zechariah 4:6 NKJV).

So understand that the fight is spiritual, and, therefore, takes place in the spirit realm, never in the natural. This applies to any area of your life that you want to take back from the devil's hands, whether it is your marriage, your children, your ministry, your finances, your career, etc.

Jesus told the disciples before He went back to heaven, "You will receive power when the Holy Spirit comes upon you" (Acts 1:8 NLT). We cannot do anything without the Holy Spirit.

I want to share something important that as believers we often fail to see and understand. Many times, we lose ground against the enemy because we do not know how to counterpunch the devil in the face. Instead of him pushing us back, we can be strong in the Lord and push the devil back.

The devil's number one weapon is persistence. Satan works very diligently to carry out his evil plan against mankind and the Church. He is very persistent in doing so. He does not take a time-out or go on vacation. By being persistent he ultimately gets the victory over his victim.

When I was in the enemy's camp, I was taught that being persistent when using evil powers would weaken my opponent and fragment their fight. The other person would end up losing his ground and giving up his turf. But I have good news to share with you: Because of the power of the Holy Spirit and the anointing God has placed on you, the devil does not have to succeed in being victorious over you. I learned how to fight in the name of Jesus Christ, to be persistent, and so can you.

The story of Samson is a great example of the devil's nagging persistence. Here is an illustration of the powers of darkness working through a person:

So Delilah said to Samson, "Please tell me where your great strength lies, and with what you may be bound to afflict you."

And Samson said to her, "If they bind me with seven fresh bowstrings, not yet dried, then I shall become weak, and be like any other man."

So the lords of the Philistines brought up to her seven fresh bowstrings, not yet dried, and she bound him with them. Now men were lying in wait, staying with her in the room. And she said to him, "The Philistines are upon you, Samson!" But he broke the bowstrings as a strand of yarn breaks when it touches fire. So the secret of his strength was not known.

Then Delilah said to Samson, "Look, you have mocked me and told me lies. Now, please tell me what you may be bound with."

So he said to her, "If they bind me securely with new ropes that have never been used, then I shall become weak, and be like any other man."

Therefore Delilah took new ropes and bound him with them, and said to him, "The Philistines are upon you, Samson!" And men were lying in wait, staying in the room. But he broke them off his arms like a thread.

Delilah said to Samson, "Until now you have mocked me and told me lies. Tell me what you may be bound with."

And he said to her, "If you weave the seven locks of my head into the web of the loom"—

So she wove it tightly with the batten of the loom, and said to him, "The Philistines are upon you, Samson!" But he awoke from his sleep, and pulled out the batten and the web from the loom.

Then she said to him, "How can you say, 'I love you,' when your heart is not with me? You have mocked me these three times, and have not told me where your great strength lies." And it came to pass, when she pestered him daily with her words and pressed him, so that his soul was vexed to death, that he told her all his heart, and said to her, "No razor has ever come upon my head, for I have been a Nazirite to God from my mother's womb. If I am shaven, then my strength will leave me, and I shall become weak, and be like any other man."

When Delilah saw that he had told her all his heart, she sent and called for the lords of the Philistines, saying, "Come up once more, for he has told me all his heart." So the lords of the Philistines came up to her and brought the money in their hand. Then she lulled him to sleep on her knees, and called for a man and had him shave off the seven locks of his head. Then she began to torment him, and his strength left him. And she said, "The Philistines are upon you, Samson!" So he awoke from his sleep, and said, "I will go out as before, at other times, and shake myself free!" But he did not know that the Lord had departed from him.

Then the Philistines took him and put out his eyes, and brought him down to Gaza. They bound him with bronze fetters, and he became a grinder in the prison.

Judges 16:6–21 NKJV

Further down in this chapter you will see that Samson's persistence brought repentance, and he cried out to God. At the end of his story, he destroyed the Philistines and got the victory:

However, the hair of his head began to grow again after it had been shaven.

Now the lords of the Philistines gathered together to offer a great sacrifice to Dagon their god, and to rejoice. And they said:

"Our god has delivered into our hands Samson our enemy!"

131

When the people saw him, they praised their god; for they said:

"Our god has delivered into our hands our enemy, the destroyer of our land, and the one who multiplied our dead."

So it happened, when their hearts were merry, that they said, "Call for Samson, that he may perform for us." So they called for Samson from the prison, and he performed for them. And they stationed him between the pillars. Then Samson said to the lad who held him by the hand, "Let me feel the pillars which support the temple, so that I can lean on them." Now the temple was full of men and women. All the lords of the Philistines were there—about three thousand men and women on the roof watching while Samson performed.

Then Samson called to the LORD, saying, "O Lord GOD, remember me, I pray! Strengthen me, I pray, just this once, O God, that I may with one blow take vengeance on the Philistines for my two eyes!" And Samson took hold of the two middle pillars which supported the temple, and he braced himself against them, one on his right and the other on his left. Then Samson said, "Let me die with the Philistines!" And he pushed with all his might, and the temple fell on the lords and all the people who were in it. So the dead that he killed at his death were more than he had killed in his life.

Judges 16:22–30 NKJV

Do the math: Persistence in the enemy's camp plus persistence in Jesus equals "victory" for us saints because Jesus Christ is all-powerful and the devil is not. We must go on the offensive with unquenchable persistence.

Are you ready to use the Word of God to stand in the face of the devil and get your victory?

These are our weapons to take back what the devil has stolen from us—our lost turf (the devil loves spiritual real estate). God used many weapons in the Bible against the enemies of His people, and I will show you a list you can use when you pray, applying it with faith against Satan and his demons. Remember that the powers of darkness hate the Word of God.

This is the ultimate prayer to set up the enemy and position yourself to get the victory:

Devil, listen to me. [You are addressing him to get his attention; you are not playing but came to fight, and you are positioning yourself for your victory.] I am attacking you from my position of authority seated with Jesus Christ in the highest of the highest heavens. [That means you are not fighting him on his turf.] I release the thunder of God against every target that has my name on it in the enemy's camp: Be destroyed now! I release the rod of God to torment every demon that has been assigned against me. I release the plagues of Egypt on the head of every devil that is trying to steal my anointing, my purpose and my destiny. I send panic into the enemy's camp that confuses their languages so that they will attack one another and so there will not be any communication of any kind. I burn down, with the fire of the Holy Spirit, their banners and scrolls that represent the assignment against me. I ask God to release angels from Michael's quarters to attack now. I send hailstorms upon every head of every demon. I release hornets to attack every devil, witch and warlock that rises up against me. I send out the hound dogs of heaven to chase down every devil and torment them, until they release my blessing. I send an earthquake into the enemy's camp to destroy and bring down every satanic altar that has been set up against me, my family, my loved ones, my ministry and all that belongs to me.

Now you can wield these seven weapons, backed up by Scripture, and take back what was rightfully your inheritance in the name of Jesus Christ.

1. The Name of Jesus

Therefore God also has highly exalted Him and given Him the name which is above every name, that at the name of Jesus every knee should bow, of those in heaven, and of those on earth, and of those under the earth, and that every tongue should confess that Jesus Christ is Lord, to the glory of God the Father.

Philippians 2:9–11 NKJV

2. The Blood of Jesus

And they overcame him by the blood of the Lamb and by the word of their testimony, and they did not love their lives to the death.

Revelation 12:11 NKJV

3. The Word of God

"Is not My word like a fire?" says the LORD, "And like a hammer that breaks the rock in pieces?"

Jeremiah 23:29 NKJV

4. Speaking in Tongues

Likewise the Spirit also helpeth our infirmities: for we know not what we should pray for as we ought: but the Spirit itself maketh intercession for us with groanings which cannot be uttered.

Romans 8:26

5. Prayer

Call upon Me in the day of trouble; I will deliver you, and you shall glorify Me.

Psalm 50:15 NKJV

6. Praise and Worship

And when he had consulted with the people, he appointed those who should sing to the LORD, and who should praise the beauty of holiness, as they went out before the army and were saying, "Praise the LORD, for His mercy endures forever." Now when they began to sing and to praise, the LORD set ambushes against the people of Ammon, Moab, and Mount Seir, who had come against Judah; and they were defeated.

2 Chronicles 20:21–22 NKJV

7. Pulling Down Strongholds

For though we walk in the flesh, we do not war according to the flesh. For the weapons of our warfare are not carnal but mighty in God for pulling down strongholds.

2 Corinthians 10:3–4 NKJV

These are the weapons of our warfare, and hell does not stand a chance against them. We are spiritual snipers taking aim at the enemy's camp on any given day. The devil is defeated and he knows that. To God be the glory, through His Son, Jesus Christ. Amen.

Once you grab the devil by the throat, the next step is learning how to keep your rhythm in the fight.

11

Keeping Your Rhythm in the Fight

In this book, my heart is to help every believer understand how to walk in victory and know that the God we serve is faithful. I learned in my young Christian walk through betrayals, hurts, pain and spiritual bleeding that, at times, other believers will let you down. Once, even the leadership of my local church let me down.

It has been said that Christianity is the only army in which the soldiers shoot their wounded, and I hate to admit it, but many times this is true. This should not be, my brothers and sisters.

What kept me going when other believers "shot" me and left me for dead was the voice of God. I thank God for His voice. In the midst of spiritual darkness, with discouragement pressing in from all sides, I was able to hear His voice piercing through my dark places. My prayer is that whatever season you are in, you, too, can hear His voice.

In a nutshell, Jesus has taught me to keep the faith no matter what. He gave me these exact words, His voice piercing through the dark clouds: *John, keep your eyes on Me always.* That one simple statement was all I needed to keep going.

Today through this book I share my heart with you, and one thing I highly recommend is that you keep your eyes on Jesus Christ and not put your trust in other people. By doing this you will find your rhythm in spiritual warfare. It would be my biggest blessing if, through my writings, you learned how to keep your rhythm in the fight.

Keeping Your "A" Game

Let me share an analogy with you. In school, anyone can get an "A" if they study; the grade is not the hard part. The hard part is maintaining the "A." The same is true in spiritual disciplines. We can find our rhythm in our purpose and destiny with the Lord, and we can find that place in the Kingdom and what He has called us to do. The key is to maintain this rhythm through every season, through every storm of life, through the thunder and lightning of life and even through the potholes and valleys.

One thing I have learned through a well-known TV preacher is that any ship can make it through any storm as long as the water does not get in. In the same way, any believer can go through anything in life as long as the situation or the storm does not overtake *you*. I am so blessed to be part of the Christian family of believers and to be on your side. It is an honor to call you my brothers and sisters.

The Christian life is a process, and I have come to understand that it is not getting the "A" in the fight that matters; it is maintaining it through the Holy Spirit to get to the other side. So many people today throughout the world try to be overachievers—the best hitter in the ball game, the highest-earning sales rep, the top of their field and deserving of an award or title. How much more for us to know the value of our spiritual walk and to win the prize of the crown that is waiting for us on that day because we made it through this side of eternity and kept our rhythm and trust in Jesus?

That is where you find your consistency in the rhythm. That is the secret of spiritual warfare: to keep the fight, to maintain the "A" and to walk in consistency of the calling of who you are and what God has made you to be. Keeping the rhythm of your hand clapping with God's hand. Awesome!

In the following section I will give you the tools to keep the fight going, to keep your light burning so that you can stand in the midst of any adversity that might come your way and to expand your prayer closet by expanding your prayer life.

God's Atomic Spiritual Bomb against the Enemy

Prayer

Father, in the name of Jesus, I pray in faith, and I put on Your whole armor that I may stand against the wiles and schemes of the devil. I put on Your helmet of salvation. I put on the breastplate of righteousness—the righteousness of Christ Jesus. I put on the girdle of truth, because I know that Jesus is the way, the truth and the life. I put on the holiness of God. I put on the sandals of the Gospel of peace so I can stand on the solid rock of my salvation, who is Jesus Christ, my Lord. Above all I put on the shield of faith to quench every fiery arrow, spear and missile that the devil shoots my way.

Lord, I pick up the precious sword of the Spirit to slice and dice with the power of the Holy Spirit, to stand all the days of my life on offense and on defense in Jesus' name.

Prayer

Father, in the name of Jesus, I ask You to keep the same hedge of protection around my family, my mind, my heart, my emotions, my ministry and my relationship with You. The same hedge You put on Job. Father, in the name of Jesus, I ask You to keep an encampment of Your powerful angels to surround my loved ones, my ministry, my family and me every day.

Father, in the name of Jesus, I ask You to send a host of ministering angels to attend to our hurts, our needs, our pain and our infirmities, to strengthen us in every season of our lives. Father, I praise You and thank You that Your glory is my rear guard. In the name of Jesus, I ask You to surround my loved ones, my ministry and me with a supernatural wall of fire. Protect me from any assault of the evil one.

Father, in the name of Jesus, I claim Your promise to be my shield and protector always.

In the unmatchable name of Jesus Christ, I command my thoughts and my thinking to be under the obedience of Christ Jesus, Amen.

Holy Spirit Fire Prayers

In the name of Jesus, the name that is above every name, I attack the devil and the demons that have been assigned to attack me in every way. I bind up every unclean spirit that is working against me, in Jesus' name. I break and destroy, going back ten generations on my father's side, and ten generations on my mother's side, any iniquities known and unknown in my family bloodline. Let them be destroyed now, in Jesus' name.

I bind up principalities and powers, rulers of the darkness of this world, spiritual wickedness and hosts in high places, and the prince of power of the air, over my region, to release and loose my family, every church in my area and myself now, in Jesus' name.

I bind up the strong man and the old man and every stronghold of every demonic spirit that is trying to plague and confuse my loved ones and me. I destroy them in Jesus' name. I bind up the spirits of infirmity, sickness, disease, pain addiction, affliction, calamity and premature death that are trying to operate against my family, my loved ones and me. I cut them at the root, never to return, in Jesus' name.

I come against, in the name of Jesus, every spirit of poverty that is trying to steal my promises and blessings. I dismantle them in the name of Jesus. I bind up the spirits of strife and division, backbiting, gossip, criticism and judgment. I smite them with the blood of Jesus seven times and break myself free from them, in Jesus' name.

141

I destroy, in the name of Jesus, the spirits of resistance, hindrance, revenge, retaliation and retribution that are trying to come against my family, my ministry and me, letting them attack one another and be destroyed in Jesus' name.

I come against, in the name of Jesus, any lying, seducing or deceiving spirit that is trying to attack me. I send judgments of God upon their heads in Jesus' name.

I bind up every spirit of fear, doubt, unbelief, discouragement, despair or depression that is trying to come against me. I ask God to send angels from Michael's quarters to destroy them now in Jesus' name. I bind up the spirits of pride, rebellion, disobedience, ego, independence, lack of forgiveness, bitterness and lust. Let them be destroyed now in Jesus' name.

I bind up any spirit of envy, covetousness, jealousy, the lust of the eyes, the lust of the world, the pride of life, the spirit of mammon, the spirits of pity and hopelessness, and every wicked unclean spirit that accompanies these spirits. I destroy them now in Jesus' name.

In the name of Jesus, I bind up every root of fear, anxiety, worry, stress, tension, frustration, disappointment and discouragement. I bind up all these devils that are working against me, in the name of Jesus.

I bind up every attack that is operating in my immune system, every affliction, every disease, every accident spirit and every demonic spirit that is trying to abort my purpose and destiny.

I bind up in the name of Jesus every tongue that rises against me, and I condemn it in judgment. I bind up every snare or trap of the evil one that is trying to operate against me, in Jesus' name.

May the Lord Jesus Christ rebuke you all.

I loose in the mighty name of Jesus Christ freedom, liberation, peace, joy, hope, gladness, love, healing, wholeness, nothing missing and nothing broken, mercy, grace, blessings and favor, restoration of all the years the locusts and the cankerworms have eaten in your life.

I loose an open heaven over your life in the name of Jesus. I loose in Jesus' name love, meekness, obedience and kindness upon you now. I loose upon you compassion, consideration for others, submissiveness and divine healing. I loose the desires of your heart, according to the purpose of Jesus Christ over your life.

I loose the blessings and promises of the Lord upon your life, family, ministry and home. I speak and loose breakthrough in every area of your life. A double portion of God's blessing be upon you, your children, home, marriage and ministry, now in Jesus' name.

In the name of Jesus, I loose promotion, breakthrough, restoration and restitution over your life. I loose a hedge of protection over your mind, over your heart and over your emotions in Jesus' name. Thank You, Jesus, always.

I speak into your life, in the mighty name of Jesus Christ, a new harvest, a new season; I speak boldness and a fresh anointing in Jesus Christ's name.

Lord, I thank You and praise You for a fresh anointing that will keep me every day of my life. I give You the entire honor, all the praise and worship all the days of my life, in the unmatchable name of Your Son, Jesus Christ.

My beloved brothers and sisters, this is how I live my life, standing and believing that God is able to keep me from falling on any given day. I trust in Jesus that this book touches and transforms your lives and brings you to a place of victory so that you will become armed and dangerous in your walk with Christ. In whatever years you have left, let them be the best years of your Christian life. I declare and decree this over your life in the beautiful name that is above every name, King Jesus.

Spiritual Warfare Prayer Guide for Everyday Life

Spiritually, it does not make sense to experience deliverance without first making peace with God. The Bible makes it clear that the only Person who can deliver you is Jesus Christ, not man. First things first—if you mean it in your heart to be set free, then you must also mean it in your heart to give your life to Jesus Christ. The Word of the Lord says,

> "When an evil spirit leaves a person, it goes into the desert, seeking rest but finding none. Then it says, 'I will return to the person I came from.' So it returns and finds its former home empty, swept, and in order. Then the spirit finds seven other spirits more evil than itself, and they all enter the person and live there. And so that person is worse off than before. That will be the experience of this evil generation."

> Matthew 12:43–45 NLT

Please do not allow any minister to practice deliverance on you unless you follow these instructions, because you will end up being worse off than when you started, and I do not want that to happen to you at any cost.

Before you do any kind of deliverance, you must be a born-again believer. That is a must. Amen.

Prayer for Repentance

Lord Jesus Christ, forgive me for all my sins. I repent in Jesus' name for every sin I committed against You and everyone else. Please forgive me and receive my repentance. I welcome You to be the Lord and Savior over my life. Use me as You will. I pray this in Jesus' name.

Self-Deliverance Prayer

Before you begin, I recommend that you get some paper towels or a bucket before you begin with your self-deliverance. A lot of these unclean spirits come out by burping, vomiting or spitting up.

Renunciations

As you pray these prayer points in Jesus' name, you will be canceling every legal right that the enemy has against you and every satanic agreement that you have made, consciously and unconsciously.

1. I renounce all agreements that I have made with Satan and his demons, in the name of Jesus.

2. I renounce and reject any satanic offerings that I have ever made, in the name of Jesus.

3. I renounce lust, perversion, immorality and every unclean spirit that I have made any pact with, in Jesus' name.

4. I renounce and rebuke all witchcraft, occult practices, divination and sorcery that I have ever made, in Jesus' name.

5. I break any ungodly soul tie in any relationship in my life, in Jesus' name.

6. I renounce and uproot out of my heart hatred, anger, resentment, lack of forgiveness, bitterness and envy. Release me now, in Jesus' name.

7. I renounce and uproot from my life every addiction, every demonic *pharmakeia* spirit that has me bound. [This pertains to the abuse of either prescription drugs or illegal drugs, such as marijuana, heroin, cocaine, methamphetamine, etc. Name the drug that has you bound, and break it in the name of Jesus.] I destroy these attacks, in the name of Jesus.

8. I renounce from my life today jealousy, pride, covetousness, self-righteousness and egotism. Come out of me now, in the name of Jesus.

9. I renounce fear, doubt, unbelief and every tormenting spirit. Come out of me now, in the name of Jesus.

10. I renounce any ungodly generational covenants that my family members on my father's side, my mother's side and my ancestors going back ten generations have made. Let them be broken in Jesus' name.

11. I renounce any allegiances to the kingdom of darkness and Satan, in Jesus' name.

12. I renounce and uproot every demonic word that I have spoken and given the devil legal rights to over my life. Be broken, in Jesus' name.

13. I renounce any spirit husband or spirit wife or any demonic spiritual divorce papers that have come into my life in my dreams. Destroy them all in Jesus' name.

14. I curse at the root every false word of prophecy spoken over my life, my family, my marriage, my children and my ministry, in Jesus' name.

15. I uproot out of my life all sickness, depression and oppression trying to operate in my life. Be destroyed, in Jesus' name.

16. I destroy all demonic activity and every demonic thought that has been opened in my life. I shut them down in the name of Jesus Christ.

17. I break off of me, in Jesus' name, any residue of any demonic kind.

18. I break off any backlash, any retaliation, any transfer of spirits that is trying to come against me, my family, my loved ones and my finances, in the name of Jesus.

Prayer to Open My Spiritual Eyes and Increase My Discernment

I thank God for the wonderful ministry He has given me, but there is no way that we can be effective in the spirit realm without having discernment and understanding in the supernatural. If you can understand the supernatural, you can walk in the supernatural; your spiritual eyes have to be open at all times. This truth is more important in our Christian walk than the oxygen we breathe. So I want to share the following prayer points with you. I know they are going to bless you—and your life will never be the same.

If you feel that anything is missing in your spiritual walk with the Lord, this is what His Word says:

> Ask, and it shall be given you; seek, and ye shall find; knock, and it shall be opened unto you: For every one that asketh receiveth; and he that seeketh findeth; and to him that knocketh it shall be opened.
>
> Matthew 7:7–8

Say this prayer with me:

O God, in the name of Jesus Christ, as the disciples prayed and asked for their faith to be increased, I know, O God, You are no respecter of persons. I pray in the name of Jesus that You will increase my faith and my discernment, and open my spiritual eyes to see in the spirit realm what You want me to see.

Prayer Points

1. Lord, in Jesus' name, open my spiritual eyes to see what my natural eyes cannot.
2. In the name of Jesus, remove every spiritual distraction and the scales that have blinded me from seeing in the Spirit.
3. O Jesus, reveal to me everything that is hidden in the spirit realm.
4. Lord Jesus, open my spiritual eyes to see all the great things that You have for me.

5. I speak into my ministry spiritual vision and revelation, in Jesus' name.

6. Holy Spirit, in the name of Jesus, let me see into the spirit realm with understanding.

7. Lord, bless my eyes to see every entrapment of the evil one that is trying to come against me, in Jesus' name.

8. Holy Spirit, help me discern the things that I do not understand and cannot see, in Jesus' name.

9. Lord, show me how to be a blessing to the Body of Christ as You open my spiritual eyes to the understanding of Your Word, in Jesus' name.

10. Holy Spirit, in the name of Jesus, reveal to me the mysteries of the Kingdom.

11. Holy Spirit, equip me with spiritual wisdom, in Jesus' name.

12. Holy Spirit, I pray for spiritual knowledge, in Jesus' name.

13. I pray in the name of Jesus, Lord, please use my gifts to be a blessing to others in my walk with You.

14. Lord Jesus, never let the light in my eyes go out, in Jesus' name.

Prayers to Function Spiritually in the Gifts God Has Deposited in Me

To us as believers in the Lord Jesus Christ, God has given a mandate here on the earth as His Church. He has equipped us to fulfill His plans, so we must understand and know the gifts that He deposited in us in order to be vessels of honor for the glory of God.

"Truly, truly, I say to you, whoever believes in me will also do the works that I do; and greater works than these will he do, because I am going to the Father."

John 14:12 ESV

When you pray these prayers, pray them in faith and believe God for the impossible for your life and ministry. Pray that your spiritual ears and eyes will be open, and that your life will be transformed by the power of the Holy Spirit in your life.

1. Jesus, I thank You for the anointing over my life.
2. I pray in the name of Jesus that I touch and agree with the Holy Spirit in every area of my life.
3. Father God, in the name of Jesus, I pray that You use me as You used Jesus Christ on the earth to heal, to set free the oppressed and to bring people to salvation.
4. Holy Spirit, I pray that You will fall upon me now in the same way that You fell upon the apostles, in Jesus' name.
5. I break and sever every demonic and every unclean spirit that is trying to contaminate my anointing, in Jesus' name.
6. Let the resurrection power of Jesus Christ rise up in me now, in Jesus' name.
7. Lord Jesus, I pray that You make me a vessel of honor.
8. Father, use me to deliver those who cannot deliver themselves, in the name of Jesus.
9. Father God, use me as an arrow in Your quiver to destroy the works of darkness, in Jesus' name.
10. In the name of Jesus, I wash myself in the blood of Jesus Christ.

11. Lord, let every demon tremble in my presence, in Jesus' name.
12. Holy Spirit, help me to stretch out my hand to touch and heal the sick, in Jesus' name.

Breaking the Spirit of Fear

In the society that we live in today, because of the circumstances and the events that are taking place, even the unbelievers are living in fear. Sad to say, I can relate to the many believers out there who are gripped and paralyzed by a spirit of fear in some measure or another.

In 1997, the devil took out my eyesight and left me blind. I remember clearly like it happened yesterday. In 2002, history repeated itself. With both of those attacks, the devil was trying to grip me and paralyze me with fear. I had to make a choice whether to believe the enemy had won or believe God for my victory. So I chose to believe that Jesus Christ was able to do exceedingly and abundantly above what I asked and prayed for.

I thank God for the victory.

> For God has not given us a spirit of fear and timidity, but of power, love, and self-discipline.
>
> 2 Timothy 1:7 NLT

For us today as believers, when we are blindsided by the enemy, whether we are dealing with a terminal sickness or divorce or even the loss of eyesight—like what happened to me—the first fiery arrow the devil releases on you is fear. When it hits you, it paralyzes. In that moment, you may even forget that you are a Christian, a believer in Jesus Christ, because the fear has the power to shake you to the very core of your spirit.

I believe in my heart that God allows these things to happen. On the other side of the spectrum, there is a small window of opportunity in which a decision must be made. Am I going to let this fear wrap around me like a python and squeeze the faith out of me? Or am I going to take the sword of the Spirit and chop its head off and take a stand, believing God for the impossible, and rise above the storm?

In my life, I have decided more than once to take the window of opportunity available to me. I was literally blind twice, and my choices at the time were, *Do I want to use a dog or a cane?* As much as I love dogs, I hated both options. Instead, I chose my window of opportunity called faith.

Prayer Points

1. I stand against the spirit of fear that is trying to operate in my life, in the name of Jesus.

2. I reject every evil report—infirmity, divorce, loss of job or loss of family member that is trying to bring fear into my life. I destroy it in Jesus' name.

3. Right now, I bind and destroy any demonic powers that are trying to take over my mind, my thinking and my heart. I dismantle them in the name of Jesus Christ.

4. I refuse to accept and operate in fear in my life. I uproot it in the name of Jesus.

5. I declare and decree no weapon formed against me will prosper, in Jesus' name.

6. Let the fire of the Holy Spirit fall upon the enemy's camp that is trying to put fear in my life, in Jesus' name.

7. In the name of Jesus, I loose my family and myself of a spirit of fear that is trying to paralyze me.

8. I come against any bad news, bad report or demonic words that will bring fear into my life. I destroy every single one in the name of Jesus.

9. I bind the spirit of fear of man, of people and of my boss. I uproot that spirit of fear, in the name of Jesus.

10. Lord, I declare over my life that You are my shield and protector, in Jesus' name.

11. Lord Jesus, no matter what comes my way, I make a decision to trust You in every area of my life.

12. I declare and decree that if God is for me, who can be against me?

13. I cover my family, my marriage, my ministry and myself in the blood of Jesus Christ.

14. I declare and decree and cover my mind and my sleep in the blood of my Savior, Jesus Christ.

Prayers to Destroy the Wiles and Schemes of the Devil

I believe that in our Christian walk we are all called to fight spiritually. But one thing we need to understand is the fight to which we are called. Many times, we get lost in the battle because the first thing the enemy does to us is to send a counterfeit fight so he can drain us spiritually. Before we jump into the spiritual ring and end up fighting the wrong fight, we must hear from God first to understand if this is truly our battle to conquer.

Let me give you an example. There have been times in my life when I have had a sharp disagreement with my daughter, and right away I categorize it as a demonic attack—especially when it happens right after I have finished a ministry event. I get into the ring with prayer at ninety miles per hour thinking that the disagreement is the result of a demonic attack, and soon I become spiritually exhausted. At the ministry event, many people were saved, set free and delivered, and the devil is not happy about that. So when I go to bed that night, the real fight shows up, but I am spiritually exhausted from the battle I fought earlier in the day. Why? Because I had gotten into the ring with the wrong fight when I could have just talked things out with my daughter.

One of the greatest things that King David did before entering into battle was to inquire of the Lord whether or not the battle was his to fight. We need to do the same today. If we do not, the devil will throw a phony fight at us, we will take the bait, and when the real fight shows up we will have nothing left to give.

King David shows us in Scripture how he got the victory:

> Three days later, when David and his men arrived home at their town of Ziklag, they found that the Amalekites had made a raid into the Negev and Ziklag; they had crushed Ziklag and burned it to the ground. They had carried off the women and children and everyone else but without killing anyone.
>
> When David and his men saw the ruins and realized what had happened to their families, they wept until they could weep no more. David's two wives, Ahinoam from Jezreel and Abigail, the widow of Nabal from Carmel, were among those captured. David was now in great danger because all his men were very bitter about losing their sons and daughters, and they began to talk of stoning him. But David found strength in the LORD his God.

Then he said to Abiathar the priest, "Bring me the ephod!"
So Abiathar brought it. Then David asked the LORD, "Should
I chase after this band of raiders? Will I catch them?"

And the LORD told him, "Yes, go after them. You will
surely recover everything that was taken from you!"

1 Samuel 30:1–8 NLT

Prayer Points

1. I ask the Holy Spirit, in the name of Jesus, to give me insight into the evil plans of the witches, the sorcerers and the warlocks that are against my family, my ministry and my life. Let them be destroyed in Jesus' name.

2. I rebuke and dismantle every plan or any insight that the devil and his demons have against me. Let them be destroyed in Jesus' name.

3. I send confusion into the enemy's camp right now in Jesus' name.

4. I send arrows dipped in the blood of Jesus Christ right now into the enemy's camp, in Jesus' name.

5. I burn down the banners and scrolls of any evil plan that they have against me and my family and my ministry, in Jesus' name.

6. I call the fire of God to fall upon the enemy's camp and destroy every demonic altar that has my name on it, in Jesus' name.

7. I call upon the Holy Spirit right now to make me invisible in the spirit realm, as well as my family, my ministry and my loved ones, so that the devil and his demons cannot find me.

Prayers against Demonic Attacks in My Sleep and Dreams

As a believer walking with the Lord for seventeen years now, I can bear witness that the worst demonic attacks that the devil has tried to infiltrate my life with came either deep in the night or when I had been sleeping.

When I was a devil worshiper, the most effective witchcraft I foisted on people took place between midnight to five in the morning, so that I could catch them off guard while they were asleep.

We have to be armed and dangerous—even when we go to bed. I remember one night in my sleep, a demon showed up in my dreams and attempted to grab me by the throat, but I kept persisting and throwing his hands off my neck. He became so frustrated that he slipped out of my dreams, ended up in my bedroom and tried to finish me off.

But thank God that the Holy Spirit had taught me how to be on offense! That night the demon's evil plans were not accomplished.

I can do all things through Christ who strengthens me.

Philippians 4:13 NKJV

He who dwells in the secret place of the Most High shall abide under the shadow of the Almighty. I will say of the LORD, "He is my refuge and my fortress; my God, in Him I will trust."

Surely He shall deliver you from the snare of the fowler and from the perilous pestilence. He shall cover you with His feathers, and under His wings you shall take refuge; His truth shall be your shield and buckler. You shall not be afraid of the terror by night, nor of the arrow that flies by day, nor of the pestilence that walks in darkness, nor of the destruction that lays waste at noonday.

A thousand may fall at your side, and ten thousand at your right hand; but it shall not come near you. Only with your eyes shall you look, and see the reward of the wicked.

Because you have made the LORD, who is my refuge, even the Most High, your dwelling place, no evil shall befall you, nor shall any plague come near your dwelling; for He shall give His angels charge over you, to keep you in all your ways. In their hands they shall bear you up, lest you dash your foot against a stone. You shall tread upon the lion and the cobra, the young lion and the serpent you shall trample underfoot.

"Because he has set his love upon Me, therefore I will deliver him; I will set him on high, because he has known My name. He shall call upon Me, and I will answer him; I will be with him in trouble; I will deliver him and honor him. With long life I will satisfy him, and show him My salvation."

Psalm 91 NKJV

Prayer Points

1. Father, in the name of Jesus, I put my full trust in You throughout the night.
2. In the name of Jesus, I will rest and lay my head down tonight in the love of Jesus Christ.
3. I seal my family and myself throughout the night in the blood of Jesus Christ.
4. I cover my home and every room of my house in the blood of Jesus Christ.
5. I cover every bed that my family sleeps on, including my own, in the name of Jesus Christ.

6. I bind every astral projecting person that is trying to infiltrate my home, in Jesus' name.

7. I cancel every demon that is trying to sneak into my dreams, in the name of Jesus.

8. Lord Jesus, let Your angels encamp around my family and me tonight, in Jesus' name.

9. I declare a wall of fire around my home tonight, in Jesus' name.

10. I pray right now in Jesus' name for the Lord to send warring angels to encamp inside and outside of my home.

My Alabaster Box

If we are not careful, history will repeat itself. My childhood and younger years—and even part of my adult life—were robbed from me because I was given over to the dark side. Today, in my travels as an evangelist, I thank God that He has allowed me to minister to so many young people in the most critical season of their lives, so that what happened to me will not happen to them.

Later in this chapter you will read letters from young people who have impacted my life. These letters mean so much to me because the young Christians who wrote them were being caught up in the web of the devil and the game called deception, as happened to me at one time. Answering their heartfelt questions and pleas for help is one of the biggest honors of my life.

In sharing these letters, I am opening up my alabaster box and pouring out something very precious to my heart. I pray these letters will bless your life as they have blessed mine. But first let me tell you how I came to receive them.

Little Boy Lost, Young Man Saved

When I was a little boy I grew up in a very dysfunctional family. The curse came mainly from my dad. My father was never loved and his dad died an alcoholic—killed by witchcraft by the witch in town. That was the story told to me by my aunt, my father's older sister. I believe my father just wanted to be accepted. In the pond of family life issues there will always be ripple effects, and somehow those will affect the innocent ones.

My father's family was never shy. They were heavily involved in witchcraft, moving up the ranks and even being hired to cast spells. Pain never wants to do right. What I mean is that you are in pain because you come from a place of torment. Pain always wants to inflict the same on others, whether they deserve it or not. So my dad's family lived, died and swore their allegiance to the dark world of witchcraft.

I told you earlier how, as a little boy, innocent and naïve, my life changed one afternoon at the house of a witch. While other kids were playing in a playground, I was being groomed in black magic. The devil became my daddy. All I wanted was to be a little boy and for my father to tell me he loved me. I wanted him to take me to the playground so we could play catch together, and for him to be proud of me in school and teach me the facts of life. Even when my dad was home, which was not often, he was still absent because he himself was never loved. How could you ever love someone if you were never loved yourself?

Sometime later in a social club, his life was terminated by a single gunshot, at the age of 33, over a woman who was

162

not even his when he had a good wife at home. The only thing I inherited from my dad was to be a warlock because he was one, too.

In 1999, at the age of 35, I had a head-on collision with the cross of Jesus Christ and bent my knee to Him as my Lord and Savior. I repented from all my sins and never looked back, and I found my purpose and destiny through the finished work of the cross. Today I am an evangelist for the Kingdom of God with no regrets. I thank God for my second chance. I want to fight for others so they can get the same chance that I received.

One Sunday morning at church I came across a dear friend who was an assistant principal of a prestigious Christian school for young people. As we greeted each other, she said, "John, I am so happy to see you. I've been praying and asking God that I would see you today."

"Hey, what's on your heart?" I asked.

She smiled. "How would you feel if the Lord permits you to come down to my school and share your testimony with the students?"

I was so excited for this amazing opportunity that the words just flowed out of my mouth. "Yes and amen," I said.

I know firsthand how the devil likes to get young people to sign up and be part of his kingdom through music, television, books or movies—at any cost. He is always looking for opportunities to destroy young people's lives as he tried with mine.

The Bible says, "The thief comes only to steal and kill and destroy; I have come that they may have life, and have it to the full" (John 10:10 NIV)

The morning that I was to share my testimony could not come any faster, and I had not slept much the night before.

I got up that morning and prayed my heart out, repeating these words: *Lord Jesus, please use me so these young people will know how much You love them.*

Flashback to a Plot Twist

Weeks before the date I was to speak at the school, though, there had been a ruckus; the devil had been trying to get his way. The enemy attacked the principal with disruption because, in the prior year, someone had shared their testimony with the students and that had brought chaos to the school— so much so that the parents of the students became outraged. Now the devil was using that precedent to try to stop me from sharing my testimony. As a precaution, the principal sent out permission slips to all the parents. It read like this:

> Ex–devil worshiper, now an evangelist for Jesus Christ, is coming to the school to share his testimony.

As I said before, God always gets the last laugh. Guess what happened? Many of the parents decided to take the day off and come to the school with their kids to hear my testimony. I knew the Holy Spirit was setting something up. That morning I had such a peace and joy in my spirit because I was going to do my best to share Jesus Christ with the young people and not to allow the devil to get his way—I was more determined than he was.

When I was escorted to the auditorium, the place was packed with students and parents. It was an unbelievable sight.

As the young people began to worship, the presence of the Lord fell upon that place, and I shared my heart right afterward. I felt the gentleness of the Holy Spirit come upon that assembly—like nothing I have seen before. I told them about my childhood and how unfortunate I was because my parents did not know any better, and how my young years were sacrificed to the devil all the way up to the age of 35. I even told them that I got married on Halloween and had a demonic wedding, and I exposed all the secrets and entrapments of the evil one and how the devil will do anything to snatch their lives, at any cost. I told them that he used television, books, music, games and other enticements to snare them into a lifestyle opposed to God.

You could hear a pin drop in the auditorium. As I spoke about the love of Jesus and the plan He has for their lives, many young people and their parents had tears in their eyes. At the end of that amazing morning, which was already ordained before the foundations of the earth, the conviction of the Holy Spirit took place.

From Nowhere to Somewhere

As I closed the service, I said, "The Bible says Satan is the god of this world, not the god of our world; we are believers in Jesus Christ. It's time to come clean." It seemed like everyone—students and parents—took a deep breath in that room. What followed was a time of repentance by the kids and parents as well. Many young people repented from witchcraft books like *Harry Potter* and *Twilight*, as well as all kinds of posters, video games, music, movies and TV programs. This was a Christian school that the devil had a stronghold on. All Jesus wanted to do was clean everyone's house to bring all these young people from nowhere to somewhere—from being victims of the devil's schemes to being armed and dangerous for Jesus Christ.

Here are the letters that flooded my inbox the week following that remarkable assembly:

October 2010

Dear Mr. John Ramirez,

Thank you so much for taking your time to come and talk to us, the eighth grade class of MCA. Your life's story and your testimony have really impacted my life. You helped me to see that some movies and music are bad for me and that they can push me to the devil's side and push me to do wrong. As a result of the change that your testimony had on my life, I ripped up my *New Moon* poster, and today I am planning to burn it. Now I plan to stay away from the ungodly stuff of the world even though I really want to see *Breaking Dawn*. My prayer is that God will be in my life forever and that I won't have any doubts about His love and power at all. Again, thank you so much!

Dear John,

Hello John, I am from the eighth grade. I just wanted to thank you for coming to my Christian academy and speaking to us. The message was a real wake-up call for me. I realize how important it is to always keep your eyes on pure things and not worldly things. You are the best preacher I've ever heard and you have inspired me to become like you. I cannot explain how much your message spoke to my heart. I could feel God touching my heart. I wish I could download that sermon and listen to it every night. When I get older I am going to read your book, but my teacher said I am not old enough now. You are a great man of God and I hope you are protected by God for the rest of your life.

Dear John,

Your testimony was great. It is awesome to hear how people were before they know God, how you felt empty and you didn't know what came over you. I love to hear those stories. You are a true hero and I thank you for coming to our school. I wish you met my dad. He wasn't at the convention, but I bet that he would like to talk to you. He was a Muslim in Iran and became a Christian in the United States. His story is really cool, too. You two should really talk. Anyone my dad talks to ends up talking to him for at least an hour. I bet you would really like him. If you want to talk to him, his number is [. . .]. He is a godly man and so are you. I really want you two to get together.

Dear John Ramirez,

Thank you for taking time out of your day to speak to us about the evils of magic. I never could have realized that *Twilight* was bad. Just seemed like a good movie to me. Now I do not want to see the fourth movie, *Breaking Dawn*. Also about Halloween being bad, I never would have thought of it that way because I just do it to get free candy.

You have really opened my mind to think about the things I watch and hear. I am no longer reading the *Twilight* stories and now I am trying to figure out what to do with my book. I hope I make the right decision. Thanks a lot for really opening my eyes.

Dear John,

Thank you for taking your time to drive from New York to our school to talk to us. I was touched when you talked about your childhood. It made me think about how other people are being healed. It also made me to be more careful about what I say, do, act, read and watch. I know better than before about how the devil can get to us. He just does not try to deceive us, but he also gets people through the things we watch on TV, books and even other people. I know that I need to strengthen my spirit, so that the only person that will talk to me is the Holy Spirit. I thank you for all that you have done.

Dear John,

Thank you for coming to our school to tell us about your life's testimony. It really means a lot to me and my fellow classmates for you to take time to come all the way from New York to our school. I can say that everyone was very moved by your miraculous story. You have given us such a drastic view on many things, and now that has really gotten deep into us. I thank you for preaching your testimony to us, for most people might find it embarrassing or would be scared, so I thank you for that. I hope God has a lot planned for your life.

Dear John Ramirez,

I just wanted to thank you for coming to our school all the way from New York. The things God has done in your life are amazing and your testimony helped many people to rethink some of their decisions. Some students threw away their posters having to do with *Twilight*; I

168

sometimes watch this TV show that occasionally talks about magic and I have decided to stop watching it. Thank you again for coming. It really made a difference.

Dear John,

Thank you for coming all the way from New York to our school. Your testimony was so powerful. I really saw how Jesus Christ can bring people back to Him regardless of what they have done. Before you spoke to us, I wasn't really sure if witchcraft was true. I had thought that it was only in certain places around the world. I had no idea that these people who do witchcraft are all around us! Thank you for making me realize that there are those kinds of people out there and that I have to have Jesus with me. What you have accomplished is so spectacular. I hope I will be able to read your book one day.

Dear John Ramirez,

Thank you for coming to our school to talk to us. When I got home, I took down any *Twilight* posters I had and put my *Twilight* series in a box in my attic. I had not realized what types of evil that these things could lead me into. Now that I know that, I am much more cautious about what I choose to read and/or watch. Thank you for taking the time to talk to us.

Dear John Ramirez,

I just want to thank you for coming to our school. You did not have to share your experiences with us, but you did. You inspired me to actually pay attention to the ungodly things I watch and listen to. Thank you so much.

Dear John Ramirez,

Thank you for coming to our school. I really enjoyed listening to what you said and was surprised and happy at the end. I am sure God would be happy, too, since He saw you and knew you would be preaching to us. When I heard the stuff about witches, I didn't know it could be that scary. They were my favorite scary things for Halloween. I guess I can't dress like them for Halloween this year. Anyway, thank you for coming. Me and my whole class really appreciate it. Bye.

Dear Mr. John,

I wanted to say that I am very thankful for the seminar you gave yesterday. It has definitely made me more critical about the things I watch, read and listen to. I want to grow as a Christian and you have showed me where I can start. I don't want to be so caught up in worldly things anymore. Although I know it will be hard, I plan to evaluate myself as a Christian more thoroughly and to make better choices in the future. I want to please God and glorify Him in everything I do. Thank you for showing me how to do that. Please continue with your ministry wherever you go. You will touch a lot of hearts. I know you touched mine.

Dear John Ramirez,

Thank you so much for coming all the way out here to talk to us about your life story. Your testimony really spoke to me about some things I need to change in my life. Hearing what you went through and how God still came through for you gave me hope. I know that what you said about witchcraft had nothing to do with me because I don't watch or do those things. But your message spoke to me in a different way. I didn't realize all the things the devil put on me that seemed harmless. But now, I am getting rid of all the bad music on my iPod, all the bad movies in my house and all the bad habits I have. So once again, I thank you for coming to share with us. Your testimony blessed me and opened my eyes.

Dear Mr. Ramirez,

Thank you for coming to my school to tell us about witchcraft. You really taught me a lot about your life. It's amazing how the Lord showed how powerful He was through a dream. You came from a third highest ranked devil worshiper in the whole NYC to a strong man of God. I want to become like you when I grow up. Thanks.

Dear Mr. John Ramirez,

When I watched your seminar, God spoke to me very deeply and I am now in the process of cleaning up my life for Jesus, like deleting all my bad songs, watching wholesome television and listening to Christian music. So thank you! No, wait! Thank God!

Dear John,

I'm thankful a whole lot that you were able to come to the school. You showed me the dangers of everything I always found all too interesting. I was encouraged to stop reading books I thought were entertaining, though now I guess I'll have to find something "more to the Lord" to read. This now to me seems like a warning about how cruel and evil wizards and devil worshipers are.

I now know what great evil can come from those people and where they may hide and try to recruit others.

Dear Mr. John,

I just want to thank you for coming to the seminar yesterday. I turned off all the demonic rock music I used to listen to. Your message really inspired me to serve God more and let the Holy Spirit lead my life. You also helped me to realize that I live in fear. I also know that now is the time to come out of the shadows of worldly things and the desires of the unrighteous, and be a radical soldier for God.

Dear Mr. Ramirez,

Thank you so much for coming to tell us about what the devil will do to the normal person like us and how he can change us. I believe what you said about getting rid of all the things that displease God. I told my mom about you and what happened to you and what could happen to all of us. My mom said that you were right about what the devil can do to one innocent person. Since I heard what happened to you, I am getting rid of all the things that will displease the Lord. My mom said she wished she had gone to hear what you had to say because she says that you are right about everything. Thank you, John, for coming to tell us your story. God bless you and your family.

Dear Mr. Ramirez,

Thank you for the wonderful seminar yesterday! It had a great influence on our class. Many people stopped watching bad movies, throwing away bad things and much more. Before you came, I didn't know that witch-craft was such a bad thing, but now I know it is a hor-rible thing. Yesterday I realized that I got ghost books from the library two weeks ago. So I went to the library and returned them both. I promised myself I will never read those books again. Once again, I thank God that you came to talk about witchcraft yesterday. Thank you!

Dear Mr. Ramirez,
Thank you for coming to the school yesterday. I really appreciate it. Yesterday when I came home from school, instead of watching *SYFY*, I decided to watch *Zoe 101*. I will try harder from now on not to watch too many of these bad horror movies or shows, like *Twilight*.

Dear Mr. Ramirez,
Thank you for coming from NYC to see us. Since you did that seminar, everyone is changing to the Lord. The girls that loved *Twilight* are now ripping their posters up and throwing their books out. Your seminar got us closer to the Lord. Now we can spread the word to others so they will join the army of God against evil. Everyone loved the seminar and came in to say what changes they made! We can tell our friends, family, neighbors or whoever else. Thank you, again. This seminar can help us in the future so we will stand up for Jesus and won't have to say, "See you in hell." It would be terrible to hear those words. Some people don't believe there is a God, and I want to try to tell them there is a real God. You have changed us by your seminar.

173

Dear Mr. Ramirez,

Yesterday when you came to our school for the seminar, it really changed the way I look at things. It has changed the way I think about God. Your speech answered a lot of questions I had on spiritual things and the demonic and the importance of God and a proper education. Your speech has changed the way I think about some of the TV shows I watch, and I thank you for coming.

Dear Mr. Ramirez,

What you said made me realize some of the things the devil shows on TV. Yesterday I was watching a movie on Disney Channel where they tried to make a teenage witch use her powers to enslave everyone. The devil tries to get us to like that junk and I really noticed that yesterday. So I changed the channel, of course. Thank you for showing me that.

Dear John,

Thank you for taking the time to come to our school and teach us about the dangers of this world. My parents and I are grateful that you were willing to share your testimony with us, and I am pleased to say that we have thrown out our *Twilight* movies. We pray for you and your family and that your testimony will continue to touch others as it has touched us.

Dear John Ramirez,

Thank you for telling us about your past and the evils that are happening today. Thank you for taking your time to speak to us. Your words really opened my eyes about what is going on in today's world. I have now realized the evils of this world and I will be more aware.

Dear Mr. John Ramirez,

Thank you for coming to our school to teach us about how bad things on TV, video, games, books, etc. are all deceiving our minds and taking us away from the Lord. I've thought about your speech and prayed to God to help me to have the strength to stop myself from watching any more movies or TV shows with witchcraft or any other curse from the devil. I will also pray for you, and once again, I thank you.

Dear Mr. Ramirez,

Thank you for coming here to speak to us about how the devil has set a trap for us, but God's love is greater. Thank you for sharing your testimony with us. After school was over, I went home and prayed for a distant family relative who was taking part in witchcraft. We appreciate you coming to our school.

Dear John Ramirez,

I am very grateful that you came to my school and shared your testimony. I want you to know that you and my teacher have opened my eyes to see the evil things of this world. Yesterday after the seminar I went home and ripped up all of my *Twilight* posters. I'm not ready to get rid of my books, but it's a process and I took a big step. I will get rid of all of my *Twilight* things and anything else that pleases the devil, and I wanted to let you know that you were the cause behind it. Thank you.

Dear Mr. Ramirez,

Thank you very much for coming to our school. I enjoyed your seminar very much. It was interesting to learn about how the devil made you do things you regret; however, God made it turn out for the better. Listening to your seminar was quite an experience. I told my mom all about it and she was grateful for your coming. My friends don't realize that everything they see or do or hear that is bad was all done by the devil. Your experience, in my opinion, has changed a lot of my friends. I read all of the *Twilight* books last year. I have to say I did enjoy them. However, after I listened to your seminar yesterday, I vowed to never read or watch another *Twilight* book or movie, or anything else with vampires, warlocks, werewolves or anything that is ungodly. I learned the devil sugarcoats things to make them seem good, even when they are not. Like you said yesterday, the grass is greener on Jesus' side. Thanks a lot!

Dear John,

Thank you so much for coming to our school and telling us your testimony. It really woke me up from all the bad stuff I was watching and reading.

The night you came to speak to us I realized that I needed to get rid of all the stuff I owned that wasn't pleasing to God. So I took out my *Twilight* poster and ripped it up into teeny shreds. I felt so relieved and happy to get rid of it. So today I am gonna burn them up too! (I really wanna get rid of them.)

Last year, someone also talked to me and my friends about how bad *Twilight* was, but I didn't listen. I just kept watching it. But when I listened to your story, I was amazed about how the devil can take things so small and make them into really bad things. I want to learn from your experience and change the way I live, and I want to help my friends do the same thing. I am really grateful for you and your testimony. Thanks a bunch.

God Has Not Passed You By

From the time they are born, our children are targets that the enemy goes the extra mile to capture. Do not be surprised at this startling reality. Instead, I hope this truth puts enough fight in you to rise up in Kingdom faith as a parent or leader to snatch your children back from the devil's clutches.

I remember being a young boy in a schoolyard on a sunny day. While playing with my friends, I noticed a group gathered in the same playground—maybe as many as one hundred people. A man dressed in a suit stood on a homemade platform and spoke to the crowd using a microphone. Whatever he was saying made the people very excited. Moments later, the man stepped down from the platform, moved through the crowd and began to pray for the people.

I stopped what I was doing and gave all my attention to the preacher. As he approached my section of the schoolyard, I became excited knowing that he would soon reach me and pray for me as well. But that was to be the saddest day of my life. As the preacher approached, he looked at me and passed me by as if I were not good enough, or perhaps he thought I was too young to make a difference.

A year later my life was given over to the devil and his demons.

What if that man had stopped and prayed for me? My life would have been very different. Everywhere I go as an evangelist, I make it my business and a mandate for my ministry to stop in every service and pray for the young people so that what happened to me will never happen to them. The Bible tells the story of the time Jesus cast a dumb spirit out of a young boy after his father begged him to set his son free (see Mark 9:17–21).

One thing you will notice as you dig into God's Word is that many of the people God called in the Old Testament were young. Esther was young, Ruth was young, Joseph was young, David was young, Daniel was young and the three Hebrew boys were young. We should never neglect or bypass young people, many of whom are in the grips of Satan because of doors that have been opened in their lives.

Pray this prayer:

Today in the name of Jesus, we serve the devil notice to loose our young people. We break every demonic attack, every tormenting spirit, every suicidal spirit, every cutting spirit, every emotional demon, every sexual demon, every rape spirit, every molestation spirit, every abandonment spirit, the spirit of rejection, every tormenting and scorning spirit of the mind— we break your powers and grip now in the name of Jesus.

Any spirit that has come in through the eye gates by watching horror movies, pornography, ungodly shows, Harry Potter *movies, Pokemon and any demonic spirits that have come through the family bloodline, we destroy your powers in the name of Jesus.*

178

Any transfer of spirits of any kind, we sever and cut you at the root and command you to leave now in Jesus' name. Any premature death spirits, lying, deceiving and seductive spirits, any alcohol spirits and any pharmakeia *spirits, we rip you apart in the name of Jesus. Leave now, in Jesus' name. Every fragmented spirit that has caused division in young people's minds, bodies, souls and spirits, we call back every piece from the enemy's camp; we call back from the north, south, east and west in Jesus' name.*

We seal our children and young people in the blood of Jesus Christ, and we release the judgments of God upon the devil. We seal every young person in the words of Psalm 91 and in the blood of Jesus, and we ask God to release angels from Michael's quarters to arrest every devil, never to return, in Jesus' name, Amen.

This is how we fight, how we cage up these devils with our God-given authority in Christ Jesus. They think they are very bright and bold, but when we come against them full-force and beat them down spiritually on their own turf with our God-given authority, they do not stand a chance.

Read the words of Jesus:

From the days of John the Baptist until now the kingdom of heaven has suffered violence, and *the violent take it by force.*

Matthew 11:12 ESV, emphasis added

Never forget that the devil loves to attack within the family because he is trying to find your weakness. Through my travels as an evangelist, I have had the honor to pray for many young people in so many places. And when I do, the devil comes at me with a rage, saying, *Look at all these young people you're praying for, and they're doing a lot better than your daughter.* The tormenting voices of the dark side come at me from every angle, spitting out lies, because everywhere I go, young people are being set free. The best cheap shot that Satan throws at me and tries to use against me is that my daughter will never have a close relationship with God as long as he can do something about it. And my daughter, Amanda, is my only child.

A Letter to Amanda

My precious Amanda,

I will never get tired of saying this: From all the daughters in the world, I am glad God gave me you. You are a precious jewel. I will even call you a diamond. Your light shines in so many ways. One of the things about you that I am most proud of is how you are so determined to accomplish the impossible. I think you get that from your daddy, not your mommy (lol). I know as a young girl your daddy left you with a lot of broken promises, and I want to say I am deeply sorry for those letdowns and for leaving you by the window. You were waiting for your daddy to show up, and he never did. Please forgive me. I am not trying to make excuses, but my mind and my heart were so black and polluted with demons. I did try with my own strength to take a sabbatical from the witchcraft world to give you the time that you deserved, and the devil punished me so severely that he took my eyesight away. But it

180

was all worth it just to think that, for once, I wanted to be a real dad to you. Thanks be to God.

Therefore, if anyone is in Christ, he is a new creation; old things have passed away; behold, all things have become new.

2 Corinthians 5:17 NKJV

I thank God that He is the God of second chances because it is not where you start, but where you finish. And this I say to you, Amanda: Even back then I would have given my life for you at any moment. That is how much I love you. I hold dear to my heart all my pictures of your birthdays and other celebrations that I was a part of, all because I loved you. And I will never stop loving you.

Today, God has given me a second chance to be a dad with a right state of mind, and I have seen God create beauty from ashes—and there is more to come. I have seen throughout the years how beautiful you are, in many more ways than one.

I leave you with this: The best is yet to come be-tween us.

Love you until the day Jesus calls me home,

Your Dad

I have learned to trust in Jesus and continue to touch young people's lives because whatever I do for someone else's kid, I know that God will do for mine. Never stop fighting for other people's families in prayer because as you take care of God's house, He will take care of your house.

I will continue to fight the good fight for the young people of this generation. I leave you with this Scripture:

But seek first the kingdom of God and His righteousness, and all these things shall be added to you.

Matthew 6:33 NKJV

P.S.

The late Pastor David Wilkerson wrote my story in his devotional time. This is one of my deepest treasures that I hold dear in my heart. Thank You, Jesus.

In Dreams and Visions
by David Wilkerson

In nations everywhere, Christ is revealing Himself to multitudes in dreams and visions. People in Arab nations, China and India are reporting their experiences with Jesus in dreams. It is even happening here in New York City.

One of our security men here at Times Square Church was once New York's third-ranking high priest in Santeria devil worship. His territory was the Bronx, and his apartment was filled with human bones. He had sold himself body and soul to Satan. But this man's heart was stirred by the Holy Spirit and he became restless. One night he challenged Jesus, "If You are stronger than the devil I serve, show me in a dream tonight."

That night in a dream, the man saw himself on a train bound for hell. It passed through a tunnel and on the other side stood Satan. The devil told the man, "You have been faithful to me. Now I'm taking you to your eternal resting place." Then suddenly, a cross appeared. At that moment, the man woke up.

He came out of that experience on fire for Jesus! Ridding his apartment of every trace of evil, he dedicated his life to

182

the Lord. Today, he is a sweet, devout man of God and is active in our church. I stopped him recently and told him, "I see Jesus in you." He answered, "Brother Dave, you don't realize what those words mean to me after twenty-five years of serving the devil." His miraculous new life had all come out of that God-given dream.

Dear saint, the day is coming when the whole world will see Jesus. The apostle John envisioned "a great multitude, which no man could number, of all nations, and kindreds, and people, and tongues, stood before the throne, and before the Lamb, clothed with white robes, and palms in their hands; and cried with a loud voice, saying, Salvation to our God which sitteth upon the throne, and unto the Lamb" (Revelation 7:9–10).

This is not a little remnant, but an innumerable multitude and they are all worshiping the Lord. Praise God for that promised day!

To God be the glory, forever, in Jesus Christ's name.

14

Waiting on God When It Seems He Has Passed You By

One of the things I have been asked so many times as a minister is what to do when it feels like God has passed you by. You clearly heard from the Lord, there were promises and blessings coming your way, you prayed and fasted, but nothing happened. You feel that you missed the blessing somehow. While your brothers and sisters in the church are getting blessed day after day, and you hear their testimonies of God's promises received, you find yourself happy for them, but also filled with sorrow in your heart.

Or sometimes you feel as if you are not even a Christian. Sunday comes and after service you go home and question yourself: *Why did I go to church today?* Deep in your heart you still love God, and you hope and pray that the next day the blessings will be waiting by your bedside. But the next morning, you find nothing but your slippers. You drop on your knees and cry out, *How long, Lord?*

Your prayers may not even be about material things: You could need healing or financial breakthrough, or maybe a promotion at work passed you by (when you thought it was yours), or you may be in turmoil when your own children are not serving the Lord. What do you do when your heart is in deep despair because you feel that the One who loves you the most has let you down?

All you hear day in and day out are the whispers from the dark side:

You are not good enough.

You missed the mark.

God does not love you.

He is angry with you.

God is fed up with you because a couple of days ago you fell into sin.

And all these fiery darts barrel at you at one hundred miles per hour. You sit in despair and unbelief while being eaten away by the devil's demonic lies.

I know what you are going through, and I want to stand with you in faith as you read through this chapter. In my own life as a young believer, coming fresh out of witchcraft, my first attack came from my eleven-year-old daughter who, on the phone, called me a traitor, and said that if she knew enough witchcraft, she would destroy me. Those words pierced my heart that day. And if that was not enough, a week later her mother called to lay down her own demonic law. She said that I could not see my daughter anymore on the weekends unless I quit attending church.

I responded, "As much as I love my daughter, you can keep her. I love Jesus more, and somehow God will work it out." Then I hung up the phone because I did not want her to hear me cry.

For eight months, on my knees, I stormed heaven. Finally, one day I received a strange phone call from my daughter's mother. The only words that came out of her mouth were: "You can have your daughter anytime you want. I don't want to mess with the God you serve."

God is good.

Crazy Faith

The power of prayer—when you never lose faith and you believe God that He can do anything—will blow your mind. I call it crazy faith. I remember one event at a wonderful church in Queens where I was invited to preach. That evening I preached my heart out like I always do, and the altar call was packed. Out of all the faces, one lady in the crowd stood out. The Holy Spirit led me to go to her and ask why she came to the altar.

"I'm a Hindu and I've got fourth-stage cancer. I'm dying," she replied.

I felt a boldness come over me. I asked, "What has your god done for you lately?"

"Nothing." You could hear the cracks of despair in her voice.

I said, "My Jesus can do two things for you today: He can save you and heal you. Do you want it?"

"Yes, I want it," she said.

That day she came to salvation, and I prayed for her healing. A year later I went back to the church and a lady was waiting at the entrance. As I walked in, she said, "Remember me?"

187

I replied, "I'm sorry, but I don't. I meet a lot of people."

"I am completely healed of fourth-stage cancer," she said, "and I'm telling everyone about Jesus—that He's the God who heals."

Later that day the pastor told me that the woman brought more people to church than anyone else. To God be the glory—prayer works.

I remember another story of a lady who came up to me at the altar and said she was diagnosed with multiple sclerosis. Without thinking I said, "That's a demon."

"How do you know it's a demon?" she asked.

God had given me a word of knowledge. "That's a spirit of infirmity, and you're under attack."

I prayed for her that day at the conference, and she went back to her home church in Canada, where her pastor prayed for her as well. Later, I was blown away by an email that she sent to the church in Baltimore where I was ministering in next. The email went like this:

> That evangelist who is going to preach at your event prayed for me. Through his prayers the Holy Spirit touched me, and after my home church pastor prayed for me, the MS left me. I am completely healed.

When I got the news, I almost cried I was so touched.

The Whispers of the Devil

In my own life as a minister I must combat the whispers of the devil. I go out and preach and witness the Holy Spirit dropping in our midst and the fire of God raging. All around me people are getting saved, healed and delivered from demons, but no sooner is the event over than I find myself sitting in my hotel room, hearing an onslaught of whispers from the dark side: *You didn't do anything. You're a loser. You're not even a minister. Look at your family—some are not even saved, but you are ministering to others. Even your only child is not completely surrendered to the Lord, and look at you—you are a fool. Others are doing better than your kid.*

The voices go on and on. I may be sitting in a small, empty airport, hearing the laughter of the demons, saying, *You came here and wasted your time.* They remind me about my adopted sister, whom I love dearly. She has been a blessing to our family from the day she was adopted. Unfortunately, through no fault of her own, she was born to a mother sick with the HIV virus. In the echoes of the airport, I can hear the demons laughing. They point their fingers at me and say, *Where is your blessing? Your sister is dying while others are being healed. Where's your breakthrough? Where's your trust? Where's your faith?*

So I know what you are going through. I know firsthand when the enemy shakes your faith.

What decision are you going to make? Whom are you going to believe? Where are you going to stand? What is your reply? I have learned to trust in Jesus. I have seen too much of God to doubt Him now. I feel like Paul, who said godliness with contentment is great gain (see 1 Timothy 6:6).

It is not what the devil has to say that counts—it is what God wrote about you. The Word means everything to God, and it should mean everything to you. Let us live in it, let us walk in it and let us get to the finish line in the unmatchable name of Jesus Christ.

Do not size up your life by other people's blessings. Even though I have been serving the Lord for seventeen years, I still consider myself to be a young believer, and I have come to understand one thing in the spiritual: There is a reward for faithfulness. You can receive the blessing first and go through the backlash or persecution later, or you can go through a season of persecution and then receive the blessing later. Whatever the way the Lord wants to do it, He knows best. As for you, just be prepared and learn how to discern.

Remember what the psalmist said: "Weeping may endure for a night, but joy cometh in the morning" (Psalm 30:5).

Yes, weeping might endure for a night, but know that a night might be six months, or a year, or several years of a night season in your life. Look at our brother Job. Historians say that his trial lasted one year, but he went through hell and back and came out clean on the other side—and he was blessed double for his trouble.

God will never forget you. He knows exactly where you are.

You need to stand in the face of the devil and say, *Satan, listen to me right now. I cannot stop what you throw at me, but one thing I know: I can do something about it through my Lord Jesus Christ. And I know my God is able. The Bible says, "Now unto him that is able to do exceeding abundantly above all that we ask or think, according to the power that worketh in us"* (Ephesians 3:20). *I will stand on that Word for me and my house. I shut down every whisper, and I shut down every lie of the devil and his cronies, because the Word of the Lord says I am more than a conqueror in Christ Jesus* (see Romans 8:37), *so I resist you in the name of Jesus Christ.*

Stand with me and declare and decree these prayers over your life:

I will not entertain, I will not listen to and I will not obey your lies. And I will proclaim the blessings of the Lord upon my life in every season. I will live and not

190

die, and I will confess these blessings upon my life today for my family, for the season I am in, over my purpose and my destiny.

I profess and declare in the name of Jesus that I have the mind of Christ. I will have good memory in the name of Jesus Christ. I will have a sharp mind in the name of Jesus, because the battlefield is in the mind.

I declare peace and joy over my life, in Jesus' name. I will declare an intimate relationship with Jesus all the days of my life, in Jesus's name.

I will decree victory over my finances, in Jesus' name.

I will decree a blessed marriage, in Jesus' name. I cover in the blood of Jesus my spirit, soul, body and mind, my will and emotions. I cover my children in the blood of Jesus. I cover my job and my career in the blood of Jesus Christ. I cover my family (see Psalm 91) in the blood of Jesus Christ. I pray the Lord will release angels from Michael's quarters to stand guard in my home in the name of Jesus Christ. I cover my vehicle in the blood of Jesus from any accidents.

I ask the Lord to equip me with wisdom and knowledge, in Jesus' name. I ask Jesus Christ to fill me with the fruit of the Spirit: love, joy, peace, patience, kindness, goodness, faithfulness, gentleness and self-control.

I pray God's favor and grace over my life, in Jesus' name. I pray God's mercy over my life, in the name of Jesus. I pray spiritual hearing and spiritual sight over my life;

191

I pray that God's revelation of His love be engrafted in my heart, in Jesus' name.

I pray that God's supernatural knowledge of His truth be engrafted in my spirit and my heart. I pray that every time I lay down my head I will have good sleep, in Jesus' name. And I pray that I will fulfill my life's purpose in this lifetime, with no hindrances or delays, in Jesus' name.

Hold On, Your Blessing Is on the Way

To live on the victory side that God has promised us, we should not waver or be moved. Hold on, even when it looks like your blessing is nowhere in sight.

Look at the life of Elijah, a man who the Bible says was ordinary like you and me. But he knew how to pray, and there is a remarkable account of his life recorded in Scripture (see 1 Kings 17 and 18). In the face of demonic forces taunting him (in the form of the sorcerers of a wicked king), and the witch Jezebel and her crazy husband, Ahab, on his heels, this man prayed to the one true God to shut down the heavens for three-and-a-half years because his opposition was crying to Baal to provide rain for their crops. Elijah wanted to show the world of his generation that the God of Israel was the true and living God.

Three-and-a-half years later, Elijah stood on a mountain with his servant and he decided to pray for rain to come. This awesome man of God had not seen rain for more than three years. In other words, everything was high and dry in both the natural and in the spirit. But he prayed that day, even though there was nothing but blue skies. Not a cloud in sight.

Everyone else would have lost hope. But Elijah prayed. He sent his servant out, but he found nothing. Elijah continued to pray and then he sent his servant out a second time. The servant came back with the same news: nothing. His servant's report did not stop this man of God. He pushed and he pressed through. He sent his servant out again, and the servant came back with the same bad news: no cloud, not even a drop of water in sight. But Elijah did not give up because he had seen too much of God to doubt now. He continued to pray and to send his servant out again and again.

Finally, the servant came back and said, "I see a cloud the size of a man's fist on the horizon." Elijah knew that God never fails, and soon, the abundance of rain came.

And let it be so in your life. Let it rain in abundance.

15

Living Armed and Dangerous

At the time of this writing, I am 53 years old and I have seen and experienced many things in life; I am sure there is more to come. There is nothing in life that I appreciate more than the experiences encountered on the journey.

When I reflect back to the little boy in the cold, harsh streets of the South Bronx, I marvel at how far God has brought me. His goodness overwhelms me. I have seen so many things in this brief journey called life. As I grew up in the '70s, my neighborhood was filled with street gangs, with their flying colors draped on their backs, their names engraved on jean jackets. Those colors were something that you lived and died for.

I met some bad people throughout my journey: gang members, street drug dealers, manipulators, con artists, liars and cheaters. But the ones who stood out the most, I would say, were the gang members. Bad dudes. They had an aura about them that sent out a statement to anyone, anywhere, that they meant business—to the point that they were willing to die for their reputations or go to jail for life.

On the other side of the spectrum, when I later stepped into the world of the supernatural on the demonic side, I met some very evil people—bad dudes in the spirit realm— who played for keeps and took no prisoners. They were the devil's best kept secret, and I became one of them. I thought to myself, *This is my world and there is no other world like it—not even one that is close with these kinds of people.* I was proud in my ignorance to brag that I belonged to the satanic kingdom. We were bad dudes and dudettes, and the devil knew it very well.

On every corner, street and avenue we left our mark. But in October of 1999 my world came crashing down. So far down that I ended up in hell, disconnected from the spiritual world, to a place of no return. But even in hell, the man Christ Jesus—with all His mercy and grace—showed up. He was armed and dangerous to the core. It blew my mind.

When I woke up and came back, I became a follower of Jesus. As I mentioned earlier in this book, that is the night that I wrote out and signed a vow to follow my Lord Jesus Christ always. I have learned through my years of walking with Him, through the power of the Holy Spirit and His anointing, to be armed and dangerous.

On the Hallelujah Side

I just want to share a quick story of when my spiritual eyes were opened by the Holy Spirit to live on the good side, or as I like to call it, on the hallelujah side. I have met some incredible servants, soldiers and even generals in the Kingdom of Jesus Christ—amazing people that you only meet once in your lifetime. I thank God with all my heart that He allowed me to see what they look like. More importantly, what they live like.

Let me start with someone I have mentioned several times in this book—the late Pastor David Wilkerson. Could you give me a few minutes while I share my story about this general and his amazing journey with Jesus Christ? God knows how to make Himself laugh by handpicking a hillbilly preacher from the outskirts of Pennsylvania and throwing him into the jungle of the streets of Brooklyn without a GPS. This man of God from somewhere in the hills of Pennsylvania had an unquenchable hunger to serve Christ.

In the early evenings of his preaching days in the country, David would come home and turn on his television to watch the news. One day he made an incredible decision to turn off the news and spend more time with God, to the point that, weeks later, he decided to put his television up for sale. That afternoon he told the Lord he was going to sell his television to spend more time with Him. He told the Lord something like, "If You want me to sell my TV, You have until six o'clock to make the purchase happen."

As the clock ticked throughout the day, straining into the evening, he glanced up and saw that it was two minutes before the six o'clock deadline, and he said, "I guess God doesn't want me to sell my television." A minute later, at 5:59 p.m., his doorbell rang and there was a buyer at the door. With $100 in his hand he made the purchase.

What an awesome God we serve. Because of that, David picked up a magazine that had an article about several teenagers being on trial for gang-related murder in New York. He got into his car and took off for New York City, and his life was never the same. David Wilkerson became armed and dangerous for Jesus Christ. During his ministry, 365 Teen Challenge programs were birthed. One of the most incredible congregations on the planet, Times Square Church, which I have the privilege of calling my home church, started with members from 104 nationalities.

I can clearly remember when 42nd Street was a Sodom and Gomorrah. It was filled with pornographic movie theaters from corner to corner, and people would go to the city and sell their bodies like candy in a candy store. The drug scene was at its high. People died on 42nd Street every day. Before Rudy Giuliani, the mayor at the time, cleaned that place up, God was already busy answering the prayers of Pastor Wilkerson. He would walk up and down 42nd Street with anguish in his spirit, crying out to the Lord.

Because of one man's prayers, today 42nd Street is called the crossroads of the world. Over two hundred million tourists come to this place every year because one man decided to pray for his region. Even though Mayor Giuliani cleaned it up in the natural, it was Pastor David's prayers that brought down the walls of Jericho in the spirit realm on 42nd Street. Thank You, Jesus.

Pastor Wilkerson's book *The Cross and the Switchblade* sold about 50 million copies and has been translated into 32 languages; it is still sold around the world. Even Hollywood took note and made a movie about his story. Through his many other books and daily devotionals that are still reaching millions of people, this one man who said yes to Jesus and no to the TV has touched the world for Jesus Christ in a way that astounds me. If I were to sum up his life, I would say that David Wilkerson lived for Christ, armed and dangerous.

Two incredible women are mentioned in the Bible that few people seem to preach about these days. One was Moses' mother. What an incredible woman she was. Not only did she give birth to an awesome baby, but she defied the odds and trusted God. She was not afraid of the king and his decrees. She lived armed and dangerous, even to the point that she was willing to die to hide her baby because she knew he had a God-given destiny. Maybe she did not have a worldwide ministry, but through her son, I am sure she received credit in heaven for all that he did.

The second woman is Mary, the mother of Jesus. Mary was an innocent young girl, living in a society in which women did not have a lot of prestige. She was touched by the Holy Spirit and gave birth to the most important baby in the history of mankind—the Messiah, Jesus. She decided to defy the odds of being an outcast and to live armed and dangerous. Because of that, salvation came to the world. What an awesome story.

In the days we are living in as believers, days of lukewarm Christianity, that kind of boldness and faith is rare. Do you want to be one of those who *do* stand up to be counted? I urge you to dress up in the armor of God and live a victorious life, whether you are the person with the two talents or five. Be one thing and one thing only: armed and dangerous.

Fast-forward to today, I would like to shed light on another general that I have had the opportunity to meet. Besides Billy Graham, I would say that he is one of the most incredible evangelists of our time. This general is Nicky Cruz. He was raised in Puerto Rico, where Nicky's parents owned a house but the devil owned the lease. His parents were known in their time as two of the most powerful witches on the island of Puerto Rico, and Nicky was born into unspeakable torment.

We do not choose families, or where we want to be born or what nationality we want to be. Things happen.

Nicky's mother, according to his testimony, had a pure hatred for him, so much so that the words that came out of her mouth could destroy him. Sometime later Nicky's parents shipped him out to New York City to his brother, Frank. In the jungle of Brooklyn, he found himself initiated into one of the most notorious gangs of his time: the Mau Maus. They were the kings of the streets and they ruled Brooklyn and every other borough with an iron fist.

Out of nowhere it seemed, Pastor Wilkerson stepped into this gang-infested neighborhood. No one chose to go there—only God would send you there. And if He did, you had better make sure that you had heard from God to go there. Pastor David stepped into this hell, even though he was slapped and spit on by Nicky Cruz. At the end of his amazing story, Nicky Cruz gave his life to Jesus Christ and became armed and dangerous. To this day, he is one of the greatest evangelists of our time.

Another awesome man of God is Watchman Nee. A man of God of Asian descent lived and ministered the Gospel in Communist China in the mid-twentieth century, one of the most dangerous places to stand for Jesus Christ. It still is today. He started churches and wrote amazing books on how to live for Christ. I believe he was an apostle Paul of his time. This brave man of God spent the last twenty years of his life in prison for the Gospel, but his light never went out. I tip my hat to this incredible man. If I were to sum up his story, he, too, was armed and dangerous.

The funny thing about these awesome men and women of God is that they had one thing in common: They knew how to live for Jesus Christ. The book of Hebrews calls it the Hall of Faith, but I am daring enough to say that, in every generation, God has a book of Hebrews filled with people of faith.

My senior pastor, Carter Colon, is one of those people. He has the Holy Spirit fire in his eyes. This is a man who answered the call of God on his life, an Abraham of our time, a man of incredible faith who has become armed and dangerous. Like Abraham, he left his country, answered the call and is serving God today with Holy Spirit fire in his bones. Through his ministry, millions of lives have been transformed, even in hostile countries.

Also, in the many churches in which I have had the privilege to preach, I have met pastors and leaders who are armed and dangerous; they are part of the book of Hebrews that the Holy Spirit is weaving together for this generation. Untouchable and unmovable, they are not threatened by what the devil throws at them.

As for my own life, I have made a decision to live armed, dangerous and out of the box for Jesus Christ. I refuse to embrace mediocre Christianity. I made this decision and I do not care two cents what the devil has to say about it. When I first got saved, I took a piece of paper, and in my naïveté, I wrote a contract between God and me. It said: *I am doing life in Jesus Christ and I want no parole.*

I have too much invested in Jesus and in my walk with Him to live in doubt and fear or unbelief. He has done so much for me, and I am indebted to the finished work of the cross. If I were to sum up my journey, I would say it like this: The day I close my eyes for the last time, I will make Jesus Christ proud for choosing me. Not that I had anything to give Him, and there was nothing good in me, but grace and mercy knew my address and came for me. I am armed and dangerous to the core, through the power of the Holy Spirit that lives in me. Thank You, Jesus.

A quote from missionary C. T. Studd sums up how I live my Christian life, and you can live yours this way, too: "My prayer is that when I die all of hell rejoices that I am out of the fight."

Living armed and dangerous does not mean that you are not going to go through hell and back. Maybe you will not live on the mountaintop for long, and maybe you will spend more time in the valley of your life. You might face trials, tests and attacks because you call yourself a follower of Christ. One thing I know is that the Lord we serve will never let you down, and you can take that to the bank. So dress up and be armed and dangerous in Jesus Christ.

Our Weapons for Living Armed and Dangerous

1. Know your relationship with God and the God you serve.
2. Know your purpose and destiny, so you will not buy into the lies of the devil.
3. Know that storms do not last. Do not make permanent decisions in temporary situations.
4. Take inventory and do an assessment of your spiritual walk. Examine the season you are in and the season you are entering into so that the devil will not trip you up.
5. It is not important what the devil throws at you. What is important is what you do about it in Christ.
6. Live every day like it is your last, in Jesus Christ.
7. Become a spiritual sniper in your prayer life and the devil will not stand a chance against you.

A Heartfelt Thought

Even though the following devotional was penned by David Wilkerson, this has been my story many times.

"You're Unworthy"—The Devil's Lie

Who tells you that you are unworthy, no good, useless, unusable to God? Who keeps reminding you that you're weak, helpless, a total failure? And who tells you that you'll never measure up to God's standard?

Who tells worship team members they're not worthy to sing praises in God's house or musicians they're not worthy to play instruments of worship? Who tells ushers, elders, Sunday school teachers, volunteers, people in the pew that they are unworthy?

That's no mystery. We all know where this voice comes from—the devil himself. He wants to keep you convinced that God is angry with you.

The devil, the accuser of the brethren, reminds you of your every sin and failure. He tells you, "God can't use you until you get this figured out and make yourself worthy." Do not fall for this lie from the pit of hell.

Many people reading this message have been convinced by the devil that they are unworthy ever to be used of God. Does this describe you? Perhaps you feel unworthy even to be called a child of the Lord. You look at your life and see inconsistency and failure.

Let me confess something to you: I have never once felt worthy of my high calling as a preacher. Throughout my years of service to the Lord, I have been barraged by accusations that I am unworthy to speak for God, to preach, to teach others, to be a leader.

So the truth is, I am not worthy to write this message and you are not worthy to raise your hands in praise to God. You see, nobody is worthy—not in our human strength and power! But Jesus told us, "*I have made you worthy.*"

"For as by one man's disobedience many were made sinners, so by the obedience of one shall many be made righteous" (Romans 5:19).

This is how you live armed and dangerous.

Love you all,
John Ramirez

John Ramirez is an internationally known evangelist, author and highly sought-out speaker who shares his true story of being trained as a priest in a satanic cult (Santeria and spiritualism). In his search for love and validation while living in a harsh neighborhood of the South Bronx, John found acceptance in a new "family" of witches and warlocks who groomed him to become a high priest in their occult religion. His plunge into the dark side reached a boiling point on the night he sold his soul to the devil in a diabolical, blood-soaked ritual.

John's life continued down this dark path until God intervened through a miraculous, larger-than-life dream, revealing Himself for who He really is and literally snatching Ramirez back from the grips of hell.

For more than sixteen years, Ramirez has been teaching believers around the globe—from cities across the United States and the Virgin Islands to Germany—about the need for spiritual warfare and deliverance. He has appeared on broadcasts such as *The 700 Club*, TBN, The Word Network and The Church Channel to teach Christians, as well as those trapped in the occult, how to combat the enemy and be set free.